HEALING FROM EMOTIONAL TRAUMAS

Release the Pain of the Past
That Is Subconsciously Sabotaging Your Happiness

Marsha Kerr Talley

To Sky, my daughter and inspiration, you have been a pillar of strength for me from the day you were born, and I am forever grateful to the Highest Source for allowing me to give birth to my best friend. You are growing up to be such a compassionate child, intelligent, disciplined, and emotionally responsible. Thank you for helping me to become a better mother and person overall. I love you.

I would like to thank Light—my son. We never got to meet in this lifetime because you left prematurely. Know that your short existence made a significant difference in my life and left an indelible mark. Thank you for gracing me with being your mother for even a short time. I love you.

Contents

Preface

"I don't need to manufacture trauma in my life to be creative. I have a big enough reservoir of sadness or emotional trauma to last me."
-Sting

January 10, 2019, was burdened as one of the most painful days of my life. As I crouched over on the floor, tears streaming from my eyes and blood hemorrhaging from my body, I could only summon the power from a higher source to help me make the 911 emergency phone call. That night was not a blur. It did not pass quickly, and the memory promised to last a lifetime. That night, I experienced more than one loss, but inspiration did not abandon me even in those deaths. "Healing from Emotional Traumas" began as therapy for me, which developed into a powerful wish to coach others through the healing process. All of us have remnants of our past trapped in our subconscious. Unless addressed, these traumas will terrorize us and continue to sabotage our happiness. As the book developed, it became a process of personal healing for several emotional wounds.

Although sadness flowed from my soul and drenched my pillowcase with liquid agony, I decided to arise. I could not stay there. I could not allow grief to overshadow me or wrap me in its darkness. Instead, I learned to face my light to pursue healing. I formulated this book to improve the lives of those who have survived early childhood and adult traumas from failed relationships to sexual or domestic abuse. The goal is to offer strategies that find and support the release of trapped emotions, which contribute to the sabotage of positive experiences in our lives.

As a teacher in public education, I meet people with various ailments that affect their social and academic skills. Regardless of who you are, some events render us incapacitated. After experiencing the devastation of a bloody and painful miscarriage, I had to face painful aspects of my past that left me feeling insecure and abandoned. This book helps you clear out negative connections that may be responsible for your cycle of stagnancy and frustration. Each step presented here helped me heal during the hardest points in my life. Within my personal and professional network, others have used the same approaches to overcome their challenges.

Identifying Emotional Trauma

"Now, every time I witness a strong person, I want to know: What dark did you conquer in your story? Mountains do not rise without earthquakes."
Katherine MacKenett

Strength can be found in tribulations and resilience in trials. Although none of us can avoid suffering, our challenges shape us. As we travel through life, inevitably, we will face disappointments. When these adverse situations become too overwhelming for us to handle, it is the beginning of our emotional trauma.

Take September 11, 2001. It is a date that many recorded as the most horrific in recent American history and one they will easily forget. This single event affected people even when they were not directly in the path of terror. People recall vividly the precise locations they heard of the tragedy. Others watched in horror as the devastation unfolded on their television screens. Regrettably, those most hapless had an up-close and personal meeting with the destruction. Imagine the horror of receiving a phone call from your loved ones as the doomed airplane plunged into the towers - a painful thought fills with emotions magnified by a sense of helplessness. Nothing could stop the outcome. The feeling of powerlessness in any tragedy can be traumatic.

Traumatizing events leave an undeniable mark. It takes time and a procession of practical resources to help ease the symptoms of trauma.

1

Research shows it is not the experience alone, which creates trauma, but our reaction to what has happened. To clarify, when an unfortunate incident occurs, most people will not respond overjoyed. It is natural to assume feelings of sadness, disappointment, concern, or distrust. Ultimately, we want to heal from things that scarred us, but those emotions can evoke a host of internal problems untreated. When sadness turns into terror and unhappiness into depression, admit the issue, then work on a resolution. Since awful things happen to good people, pain is no stranger to any of us. It is crucial to be attentive to our thoughts to not cause our behaviors to pull us into a dark place.

Our immediate and gradual reaction to a painful situation, such as 9/11, influences whether it becomes traumatic. None of us will look at any situation the same, so we learn how to cope with issues to avoid emotional trauma. The devastation left some stagnant, but others use the tragedy to grow. With every decision to heal, we develop emotional intelligence to leave the destruction, set boundaries and seek help as needed.

We all deal with unfortunate events, and the symptoms of emotional trauma manifest in unique ways. For instance, men and women return home to an abusive situation daily. These individuals may look happy on the outside, but their self-esteem is shattered by circumstances and self-doubt on the inside. They go back to the person who contributes to their harm. Even with the physical bumps and bruises, they find it hard to leave. The abusive relationship causes emotional trauma; however, remaining in one is also a sign of a deeper issue. While some people feel compelled to stay in a painful relationship, others free themselves from the dysfunction. They learn how to detach from the toxicity and love themselves again.

Sometimes we are not the victims, inflicting suffering on others. Healthy individuals do not afflict others with pain. Since we know hurting people hurt people, your cruelty is a sign you need healing. Early childhood troubles can leave us broken, yet we have a personal responsibility to transform our lives beginning with a commitment to change. In writing this book, I met people who admitted to afflicted

2

others with pain. Today, they are remorseful but still do not believe they deserved forgiveness or even love because of what they had done. Regardless of what side of the pain we find ourselves—the victim or the aggressor, redemption is possible. For anything to become better, we must accept that failures do not dictate our lives. Our past does not predict our future.

Sometimes we hurt others unintentionally. Once you realize what effect your behavior is causing, you can correct it to avoid continuing the other person's anguish. However, it is not our role to ensure someone else is never uncomfortable. We all hurt. Although we understand excruciating circumstances create long-lasting effects and are much harder to "just get over," we must learn how to let go. We cannot live healthy, productive lives governed by the pains of our past. Trapped emotional trauma creates toxicity that impedes our relationships but can be detrimental to our physical health.

We are what we think as we are what we feel. Our minds and emotions can create our reality. When we attach our feelings to memories, positive or negative, we re-live that moment even though it may have happened many years ago. This book encourages you to expose those things you hid in your head and heart. Those things that have been interfering with your abilities to live a fully functional experience.

As we travel this road called life, we must learn how to manage our emotions despite the circumstances. When we are in survival mode, we are operating from the memories that caused us the most pain, and we treat people accordingly. Although we have learned how to compartmentalize our baggage well, we must address the issues. In fact, the older we get, the chances of being hurt or causing pain increases, yet the single goal is to travel life light. It is impossible to live a full life with the heavyweights from negative emotions trapped in our heads and heart. It is laborious.

Carrying around unresolved issues creates stress and produces other problems. Sometimes, those issues manifest as physical ailments, yet other times, it becomes a dysfunction of our minds. Ergo, we must

3

create habits that can detect when we need to cut ties from our allegiance to suffering. While your feelings of disappointment, abandonment, or fear may be valid, you cannot remain there. You cannot wallow in self-pity. Instead, you must fill up your life toolbox with many tools to help you dig yourself out of the shallow grave you dug yourself. Today, become the love you deserve one decision at a time.

Mary Manin Morrissey, a motivational speaker, life coach, and creator of the DreamBuilder Program, states, "Even though you may want to move forward in your life, you may have one foot on the brakes. To be free, we must learn how to let go. Release the hurt, release the fear, and refuse to entertain your old pain. The energy it takes to hang onto the past is holding you back from a new life."

Character is the mental and moral qualities distinctive to an individual which hardship nurtured. We learn who we are in hard times. We discover our potentials in discomfort, out of our comfort zones. While none of us chose devastations, we can use them to motivate us into our purpose, turning pain into passion. How many people of significance do you know who produced their best work following heartaches? Likewise, do not allow what has happened to you to define your potential. Instead, use those learning curbs to propel you into servitude and become your best self. Life has several tools for building our resistance, through the fire, the rain, and the sunshine. Even when things go well, learn something new about yourself. Our human experience is not just about suffering and pain. Use them all to unleash your greatness. Life is getting what you want and enjoying it with those you love the most. While someone may have intended the worst, you have the power to transform that situation into something that works for your good. Life can become your wonderland.

Remember, you have survived 100% of your worst days. While you will never want to repeat the woes of times past, remain grateful for the enlightenment. There were days you felt you would not make it. You had no more strength. You cried your last cry, and you were empty. Nothing suggested that you could rise again, but a glimpse of

4

hope shows up. You have today, and there is more. Today, you have inspiration stirring within your belly. You have found a new push inside of you, and you are ready to try once again. Push through. You have already come this far so you can live. You can thrive. Decide right now you are not your past. You are not a product of what has happened to you, but you will be productive with your decisions. Maximize your pain. Look at the situations of yesterday, release the bad feelings, forgive the person who wronged you, and use those circumstances to motivate you. You are enough, so become the love you seek one decision at a time.

Turning Suffering into Significance

Oprah Winfrey, renowned for her Oprah Winfrey Show and so much more, is a most influential woman. They ranked her talk show the highest rating television program of its kind in history. Knighted as the "queen of all media" with the Midas touch, she became the first African American multi-billionaire making her the richest of the 20th century. However, like many great ones, her story did not start as a beautiful one. Instead, pain and misfortune seemed to lace her early years. Winfrey was born in poverty, raised by a single mother, and her father lived out of state. She survived sexual molestation early. At 14, she became pregnant; later gave birth to a son born too early and then died two weeks postpartum.

If you have never experienced the fear of giving birth to a child before full-term or having a child die, you can only imagine the utter devastation. There is nothing as upsetting. Now, imagine being a young teenager going through this. One can imagine this was a traumatizing time of her life. If it was not, I could see how agonizing this period of her life must be for her, but she did not succumb to the weight of all those factors nor became a victim of circumstances.

Winfrey used those disasters to fuel her. She discovered her voice and used her talents to heal so many others while facilitating her own. Her story is remarkable that has inspired many worlds over, including the girls of her Oprah Winfrey Leadership Academy for Girls in South Africa.

When nothing goes right in our lives, it feels like life is against us. Besides the physical pain coming from what is happening, there is a sense of loneliness, which provokes emotional fatigue that can cause additional stresses. All of this can conjure up reminders of past traumatic experiences. When this occurs, it is a reminder we must release those pent-up emotions from our heads and hearts. Someone says stress is a silent killer because it almost simulates an infestation within our bodies that can harm us if it goes unattended. It is a symptom of unreleased emotions. We must become healed from emotional traumas to facilitate living our best lives.

Quick Write:

After being molested, I determined never to be someone who allowed others to intimidate or belittle me from a very early age. Growing up, I saw men use and abuse women, so I resolved that I would become no one's victim. When people said I was aggressive or behaved too assertive, I took it as a compliment. Although I had grown from my vulnerabilities, there were humbling moments where I could not rely upon my strength.

Think back to a time you felt depressed. What did you do to get out of that state? Include in your response the people who helped you through it.

_____

_____

_____

_____

_____

_____

_____

_____

_____

_____

_____

_____

Summary and Key Takeaway

This chapter reminded us that adversaries are occasions to become more resilient. In the words of Iyanla Vanzant, "It's possible to turn the most upsetting situations into opportunities for growth if you can muster enough willingness, trust, faith, patience, and surrender." Learn to turn terrible experiences into something beautiful.

Next, we will discuss emotional trauma, and some of its root causes are. This next chapter is a significant portion of the book that may conjure up negative memories. Later, we will address how to release those emotions to live a more fulfilling experience.

I.   What is Emotional Trauma

"There are wounds that never show on the body that are deeper and more hurtful than anything that bleeds."
— Laurell K. Hamilton, Mistral's Kiss

We are all familiar with physical trauma. When we hear the word, trauma, we visualize someone with a gushing wound accompanied by excruciating pain. The same is true for emotional trauma, except it is unseen and only evidenced by symptoms, such as anger, drug addiction, depression, or promiscuity. Everyone deals with trauma in different ways. Some people ignore it, some make light of or justify it, while others desire to heal from it. If you have experienced a stressful event that left you feeling helpless or out of control, you may have been traumatized. How you address this internal laceration will determine your quality of life and the health of your relationships.

Psychological trauma can leave you struggling with upsetting emotions, memories, and anxiety that will not go away with just time alone. It can also leave you feeling numb, disconnected, unable to trust. (Emotional and Psychological Trauma, n.d.) Worst it can cause you to act out and take part in regrettable activities that hurt others as you repeat a sick cycle of maiming yourself. When sad things happen, it can take a toll on a person's confidence. With patience and the right strategies, the road towards personal recovery seems more encouraging.

Do what is necessary for your mitigation, stay the course, and respect the healing process. For a period, you must consciously take part in activities that recreate habits to restore soundness to your state of mind and bring happiness to your heart. Take your time without the temptation to rush through the pain. Avoidance will not work. Just because you do not address an issue does not mean you have healed through it. Whether the trauma happened years ago or yesterday, it is possible to release the negativity that has impacted your life to create healthier experiences.

Emotional trauma occurs with constricted feelings. It is one you ponder on often, or it plays in your being's background without you realizing the impact on your behavior. Sometimes, the wrong thing happens at the wrong time, causing a simple situation to be monumental after several other disappointments occurred.

For example, if you just lost your job, struggling to pay the bills, then your partner breaks up with you, the last event may take the most toll on you, leaving you aching and feeling crushed. In isolation, those occurrences may not have been a problem, but they become overwhelming in combination. Thus, it is not the event alone that makes it traumatic, but its overall effect on how it makes you feel. Any extraordinarily stressful event, whether or not it is physical, could cause trauma.

Regardless of what we face, how we address the issue will ultimately influence the quality of our life. While none of us may hurt on purpose, we can prolong the pain by refusing to adequately deal with it. It is up to us to use the right principles and practices to overcome challenges. It is up to us to exercise courage to face those things that make us feel awkward, unworthy, or downright ugly to move towards our inner bliss.

There are things we conceal in the inner chambers of our hearts, hoping that out of sight will mean out of mind. Emotional trauma does not work like that. Even though you may have forgotten about it, the remnants of the distress do not go away. Avoiding it may bring some level of ease, but it will not bring healing. Those memories do not just disappear but linger in the background, playing on a loop in our subconscious. You can tell this is true because of how quickly you have gotten upset over seemingly innocent situations. Think about it. You get so easily triggered by certain things people say or do. We question why we keep having the same relationships. We wonder what makes us do the same things over again that we said that we would not do.

Although your reason for indicting someone else may be valid, that alone will not remove the trauma or solve the emotional problem. Instead of blaming anyone else or disregarding the evidence of something deeper happening, we must learn how to heal from what has hurt us. That is a hard pill to swallow when you must become responsible for what someone else may have done.

Trauma and Gender

There is a distorted perception that many perpetuate about men regarding emotions. They do not have as many as women. Studies show they have the same amount with varying degrees of emotionality and emotional constriction. Research suggests that men have more trapped emotions than women. These are emotionally traumatic events that they have yet to address. Keeping hurt emotions pent up has direct links to posttraumatic stress disorder (PTSD). (Valdez & Lilly, 2012) While we are familiar with people returning from combat suffering from PTSD, this disorder is not just related to soldiers. Those who remain in abusive relationships or refuse to deal with traumatic events can show similar symptoms from this emotional and mental impediment. It would appear then that while men may experience the same emotional traumas as women, they deal with these feelings differently that may later contribute to toxic behavioral patterns.

The inability to deal with your past can appear your ability to thrive in your present situations. Despite a desire for healthy relationships, many of our encounters involve people from broken families with a history of childhood abuse, displaced anger, and an inability to grow from what has caused them pain. These attributes, combined with our maladjusted traits, can create distressing situations and unfortunate results. Once we see a pattern of misaligned outcomes, bad behaviors, or poor judgment, it is up to us to do what is necessary to resolve the internal conflict.

11

In my book, "Men Need Self-Love, Too," we will explore the issues men face that affect their relationships from a boy into manhood. It highlights the testimonies of those who have overcome childhood abuse struggles and toxic masculinity with a strong emphasis on their side of every story.

Psychologists show that a father's role is one of the most important in a young girl's life. He becomes her first role model, establishes the standards on which she perceives herself, and teaches the treatments to accept from others. Fathers play a significant part in their daughters' views on men. This father-daughter connection may impact or impede her intimate relationships. Active and present fathers promote a healthy sense of self and avoid unhealthy relationships with other men.

While we would like to look to our parents for a great start in life, they were once children, and many experienced troubles that contributed to their dysfunctional sense of self. Experts claim that absent fathers create self-esteem and other emotional issues. In retrospect, too many of my relationships with men involved some level of anguish. It was not until much later that I made any correlation to my father. Active and present fathers promote a healthy sense of self to facilitate healthy relationships, platonic or otherwise. The same is true for boys.

Unfortunately, too many of our fathers were broken themselves and indirectly contributed to a dysfunctional sense of self. Experts claim that fathers who are emotionally or physically absent create self-esteem and other emotional issues.

We have heard some say women choose men that are like their fathers. There is some truth to that saying. As an adult, I discerned that I looked for specific characteristics in the men I dated. I wanted what I liked in my dad or what I missed out on in my childhood—effective communication, sound advice, consistent consideration, warm affection, and an overall sense of security. Although I yearned for these qualities from my partners, the men I met rarely exhibited all these skills. Since I continue to seek an overall sense of security from men, I felt that my relationship with my parents affected me, but I did not consider to what extent.

Childhood and Trauma

E motional trauma happens when we harbor negative feelings and obsess over what went wrong. It may cause us to blame others for our actions and subsequent character flaws without considering that everyone has their burdens to bear. In my self-analysis, I discovered that I had unresolved issues with my father that I had to rectify. My father worked hard, spoke little, and showed fewer emotions. His number one priority was to be a provider and ensure that we were clothed, sheltered, and fed. Even though he had never told me that he loved me, providing for my basic needs met that he did. I genuinely believed that he did the best he could. Despite that understanding, as I reminisced over my childhood, it perturbed me that I only recalled being hugged by my father once.

Unknowingly, instead of letting go of the disappointments over time, I locked them away in the chambers of my heart to never again revisit, but they were not gone. As expected, my early childhood traumas affected my personality and influenced how I perceived people. I always expected someone to let me down and never had a real sense of belonging. Writing this book reinforced the importance of not scathing over issues. There was a wound inside me that needed to be addressed and dressed

My parent's marriage ended in divorce. Unbeknownst to them, one of my first memories of them involved domestic violence. I could not have been more than two years old. Interestingly, throughout the years, I had never held my father responsible for any of the mishaps in my parent's relationship. Somehow, I thought he was justified without considering what he had done to contribute to his marriage's mishap to my mother.

After my father left home, I felt it was my duty to protect myself, so I became more assertive at a very young age. I was unintimidated and unafraid of expressing myself. That year, I turned six. It was a pivotal time in my life. My mother started dating again, and I was violated by a man whose name will remain unsaid. That incident left an indelible mark on me. Even though I have grown from that place, it has remained one of my most traumatizing moments. It was also the defining moment when determined never to become a victim. Instead of withdrawing into a shell, I became even more resolute.

Over the years, that scene of assault replayed in my mind. I questioned everything and pondered why a grown man would force a six-year-old baby into a sexual act. Three decades later, I am still trying to make sense of it. Thinking back to that day is dark. The only glimpse of brightness comes at the thought that I fought back - a child biting and gnawing at an adult to get off her. Each time I revisited that place through my mind's eyes, a renewed sense of abandonment washes over me. For a long time, I felt betrayed by my mother and faulted her for what had happened. In time, I learned to forgive and thought I had let the hurt go. Instead, those childhood feelings did not subside. Instead, they grew into emotional tumors locked away in hidden places.

As far back as I can remember, I have had to fend for myself. Survival was a mechanism, and the tendency to be defensive became second nature. I did not see the world with naivety because I was exposed to distresses in life prematurely. Being a survivor of a childhood sexual assault, I had developed resilience and prided myself on the ability to protect myself. However, through self-discovery, I realized that I was still angry. Angry at my mother. Mad at my father. Furious at the man who caused the violation. I was even mad at myself for not being able to make better decisions, and that anger showed up in many ways that also affected my perception of self. Despite my growing confidence, I struggled with the idea that I had would experience love without conditions. Additionally, I often anticipated something going wrong whenever something good happened.

Victims of abuse, any abuse, must resist the urge to repeat the cycle of mishandling children, especially. Hurting people tend to hurt people, and often children are an easy target to unleash unresolved anger. Through the growing pains, I became adamant about not being a product of my environment or repeating the same affliction on my daughter, so I decided to be a different kind of mother. Because of my conditioning, it was not always easy to resist the urge to be verbally or physically abusive. Still, I was committed to giving my daughter the love and security that I desired as a child. To do this, I had to change my mindset, adjust my core beliefs regarding discipline, and handle my emotions.

> ## "I cannot think of any need in childhood as strong as the need for a father's protection."
> - Sigmund Freud

My marriage ended in divorce. As the resilient, well-rounded, and resourceful person I could be, the men I attracted seemed incapable of treating me well. Their admiration soon turned to dismissiveness or deviousness. Either I intimidated them, or they saw me as a challenge to conquer. Only a few reciprocated. Although none of them had identical personalities, there were some commonalities. I do not believe they were trying to hurt me, but each time something awry happened, my disappointment compounded, and I blamed myself for their behaviors. I was the common denominator, so I believed that I had a part to play in infidelity, manipulation, emotional abuse, or neglect.

There is a saying you teach people how to treat you. Because it is irrational to believe that someone would teach others to mistreat them, this statement alone is faulty. A complete explanation is that we show people what we will tolerate by what we accept. Although we are not responsible for how others treat us, we have a part to play by what we continue to endure. A person with integrity, will act out of integrity even in situations where he can act less because that is the nature of that person. With time, though, he could learn from you that acting and unkind will still be acceptable, which could influence how he behaves.

For instance, observe school-age children. Even though students know the general expectation of how to behave in school, they will try every teacher whose class they are learning what they can get away with in there. They understand that standards and expectations change from teacher to teacher, depending on what that specific teacher allows. In one class, a student knows he cannot get out of his seat without permission or use profanity, but that same student will be most disruptive and disrespectful in another. They learn the misbehaviors and will continue whatever the actions are reinforced or rewarded.

The first time I experienced infidelity in my marriage, I did not get angry. Instead, I was consoling at the expression of remorse. In my naivety, I believe that to be the last time anything compromised our union as man and wife. It was not. While I was being considerate in taking time out of my day to work through what happened, it was indirectly teaching him that I was strong enough to deal with it again. My sympathy enabled his decision for future misconduct.

Consciously, I was not teaching my spouse to cheat on me or continue to betray my trust, but I showed one more thing I would tolerate keeping my marriage intact. As time passed and the reoccurrence increased, he took less responsibility for his actions and soon began to blame me for doing what he did. Inadvertently, since I had forgiven him and stayed instead of deciding to walk away, I taught him it was all right to behave in this way without consequences. Someone planted the mindset to personalize what others do within me long before I even knew who I was as a person or how I should act as a wife.

Relationships take work. With experience, we realize that building anything; it takes effort. That was one reason I stayed in situations which became toxic. I did not want to be the person who quit prematurely, so I gave everything and bore many things before finally deciding to walk away. After watching my parent's dismantled union, having a tumultuous marriage of my own, and knowing my father

16

remarried twice more while my mother did not, and other failed relationships, I sat down with a counselor. Together, we discovered that I had deep-rooted issues stemming from those early memories and my family dynamics. During a counseling session I grasped the truth I had no real example of what a healthy relationship looked like outside of literature or the media - a daunting realization.

Twelve was a significant age for me. I started my period, was in my first year of high school, and it was the time something compelled me to tell my mother what had happened to me at six years old. I remember that evening like the back of my hand. Not only did she not believe me, but she also blamed me. As others witnessed the argument unfold, it was them that came to my support. Instead of relief, she called me a liar, and I had to defend myself against her further. Interestingly, this situation was equally traumatizing as the actual molestation. Now, I can understand how trapped emotions within us can contribute to regrettable actions or reactions.

It was not until I became deliberate about healing from past hurts that I began to unearth the problems I had with my feeling of neglect that backed to my childhood. I had locked them away, but they were still sabotaging my present-day happiness. Maya Angelou's "As the Cage Bird Sings" relays a similar story. When I read it, I could not stop crying because it conjured up the anguish of that dark day. Like Angelou, though, I had a determination to turn pain into a passion.

We all learn the coping mechanism necessary for managing our life's disappointments. For me, I remained assertive, but my optimism slowly became a little more skeptical. What I have realized over time is not to invalidate my experiences because someone else's maybe worst.

I remember one time I cried so hard that it felt like my belly would fall out. I had locked myself inside my closet and wept for what seemed like hours. Although a heartbreak triggered the breakdown, it was mostly of compounded emotions of all the times I needed my family, and they were not there. It was grief—deep grief for all those years of reliving the abuses, physical, sexual, and emotional. It was sorrow for

17

all the time someone had let me down. It was heavy. It was the tears of the child inside me left alone and lost, yet it was her responsibility to find her way. I desperately needed a fortress. Somewhere that I could feel safe with just one person whom I could trust. I had not met that person, so that moment, that man was the catalyst for all the bawling. Unbeknownst to me, this was evidence of emotional trauma.

The way I perceived myself through those events created patterns I continued to repeat year after year. However, the time came when I just wanted the freedom to be the best person I could be. I wanted to be a healthy and happy woman, regardless of my relationship status. I wanted to be fully content in whom I was becoming without every lingering presence of self-doubt, so I could no longer use my past to justify my behaviors. Healing to grow became the focal point of my personal development. I could not wait for my mother to accept her role in my conditioning. I could not ask my father to be more compassionate, nor could I force those men to treat me with care. I had to recognize that this journey was a personal one.

II.   Causes of Emotional Trauma

"Someone was hurt before you, wronged before you, hungry before you, frightened before you, beaten before you, humiliated before you, raped before you... yet, someone survived... You can do anything you choose to do."
—Maya Angelou

An unfortunate event alone does not make it traumatic. How a person reacts to a situation depends on several variables. People are more likely to become traumatized by a distressing situation when they are already stressed. They have suffered a series of unfortunate events, including losing loved ones, or experienced trauma early in their childhood. Although many of our issues as adults began in our early years, some developed crises as we grew into adulthood. It is essential to identify the cause of the symptoms of trauma and address them with the steps that will allow us to overcome the pain to facilitate healthy relationships with ourselves and others.

Stress

Stress, whether physiological or biological, stress is a person's response to a stressor such as an environmental condition or an unfortunate event. Stress is the body's method of reacting to a situation such as a threat, challenge, or physical and psychological barrier. Various systems in the body respond when stimuli alter our environment. The autonomic nervous system and hypothalamic-pituitary-adrenal axis are two major systems that respond to stress. (Stress, n.d.)

Stress and illnesses have a direct link, and none of us is a stranger to it. However, for me, there was one year where stress manifested itself into a severe health concern. During that time, work was intense, and life at home was troubled. I felt like I was at the point of burnout. My body started to create signs telling me I needed to get back in alignment with everything going on. I passed clots, and my cycle was longer than usual, which brought me to the doctor's office. There, they

diagnosed me with high blood pressure and chronic kidney failure —
devastating news since my life centered on health and wellness.
The pressure at work, my relationship with a man that suffered from
OCD tendencies, who also seemed hell-bent on demeaning me at
every chance he got, were proving to be entirely too much for my
body. Earlier in the book, we introduced the idea that one incident
may not cause trauma, but when compounded with other struggles, it
might. It took a toll on my overall sense of self, and I felt the pangs of
being worn down. The physical ailments were symptoms of emotional
trauma.

I did not leave the first time his bad behaviors showed their cruel head.
Instead, I stayed, hoping my love and patience would encourage him to
change. They did not. I always felt conflicted. On the one hand, I
presented this message of intolerance for anything less than deserving.
I always encouraged others to pay attention to red flags, but then in my
personal life, it would appear that I was living a lie. I was taking it at
home. I had become a hypocrite, and I was miserable. I began to doubt
myself and slowly started to go into a state of depression. Besides my
internal conflicts, it also worried me about the example I was setting
for my daughter. I never wanted her to accept abuse from anyone or
receive it as love. While I wanted to teach her to work through
problems in her relationships and not give up at the first sign of a
challenge, I also did not want her to believe that this was an example
of a healthy relationship. It was not.

The culmination of events and their prognosis helped me realize that
stress kills, not figuratively but literally. The doctor prescribed 50 mg
of metoprolol, 25 mg to be taken twice a day. Before that moment, I
took no medicine, not even contraceptives. It was all too
overwhelming. Along with the prescription, the doctor recommended
that I took time off work because they determined it to be far too
stressful for me. I was on medical leave for two months.

Honestly, since I am a strong proponent of natural remedies, I struggle
to heed to my physician's medical advice. Convinced that reducing my
stressors could ease my health problems, I started to make some

immediate changes. First, I had to be intentional about not stressing out, then I increased my water intake, reduced the sodium in my diet, increased my exercise routine and sauna visits. I bought a blood pressure machine to monitor how these modifications helped my blood pressure. I kept a watchful eye on my blood pressure using a monitor. Besides not being in the classroom, the changes helped. After three months of my focused, healthy lifestyle and without the dependency on the drugs, my doctor told me I did not have to take them anymore. I was elated.

Despite my excitement for the new school year, it began with news that a man she loved had murdered my cousin, Simonne Kerr, in cold

blood. She was just younger than me, who worked as a nurse and was a mother still recovering from her only child's death. My daughter and I spent the entire summer before his death with them. Learning he killed her and in such a violent way upset me to the core. So much so I was numb. I did not want to acknowledge it. Since she lived in England and I lived in America, I would pretend that we just

Figure 1 Simonne Kerr and me after the death of her son, Kavele.

had not spoken for a long time instead of considering her dead. I could not bring myself to accept that yet.

My blood pressure spiked high again, and the doctors worried about how I could function with stroke level BP numbers. My doctor now wanted me to be on the medicine for the rest of my life. Stress had once again triggered this hereditary disease, so now my body was having a harder time adjusting to challenges that I had faced better before. I was not dealing with them well, not mentally, not emotionally, not spiritually, not physically. I was not coping well. After

21

releasing another large blood clot, I was again in the obstetrician-gynecologists office. I was pregnant — this news was bittersweet.

I wanted a baby, but the relationship between my partner and me had changed drastically, so I questioned keeping the pregnancy. Having this child would mean a lifelong connection to him, but I longed for an exit plan with all that had happened. I no longer wanted to be tied to him at all. I even battled with the idea of abortion but determined that it was against my moral and spiritual values. Besides, I convinced myself that this child was a blessing regardless of the outcome with his father. I called him Light. Three months later, I had a miscarriage.

Though the doctors tried to reassure me that this was a common occurrence, I remained convinced that the blood pressure medicine combined with the overwhelming stress load contributed to his passing. From that moment, I was determined to get my health back into my control. I could no longer allow anyone or anything to risk my health. It was time for a drastic change. Letting go of haunting memories takes work. It is an act of self - awareness to recognize when something sinister operates below the surface. Many of us do not know how to address what caused the distress. Instead, we bury our thoughts or even block out any recollection of what happened. Unfortunately, research has shown that ignoring the pain does not make it go away. Instead of avoidance, we become purposeful about healing. I planned to get through the turmoil one decision at a time.

Pregnancy Loss

For many, pregnancy is a time to celebrate. Parents and loved ones are excited as they anticipate a new baby. From the beginning, the mother bonds with the growing baby, and the father gets ready to be a dad. Even though the doctor warns against sharing the news with others until the end of the first trimester, the air is buzzing with good news, and most expecting parents find it hard to keep the secret. The feeling you get from creating a life with someone you love is like none other. All preparations are now for the safe arrival of the baby. As a mother, you are cautious about what you eat, what you drink, how hard you work out, lifting heavy objects, and almost every waking thought centers on the baby.

For some women, that bliss is short-lived. A miscarriage is a spontaneous loss of the baby before the 20th week. The feelings of joy become replaced by devastation and blame. Even the physical symptoms of bleeding, the excruciating pain, tissues and clots passing through your body, severe abdominal cramping, and weakness do not compare to the extreme sadness that mothers feel combined with an overwhelming sense of guilt.

"Miscarriage is the most common complication of pregnancy in the United States, occurring in 15–20% of clinically-recognized pregnancies, or 750,000–1,000,000 cases annually. Despite its frequency, miscarriage remains shrouded in shame and silence, even amongst friends and family, and its emotional impact has not been sufficiently investigated." There is an overwhelming sense of self-criticism that comes with a pregnancy loss. Without proper support, it is easy for a mother to slip into depression.

The simplest things can cause tears, not just shallow crying but all-out bent over bawling. The thought of losing your child is excruciating regardless of his stage of life. All the planning and preparation for the grand arrival are now reminders of what has gone. Surviving a miscarriage can be awful. According to a survey conducted in 49 different states between men and women, 64% thought stressful situations caused pregnancy loss, with 47% feeling guilty. Overall, those who had experienced a miscarriage felt guilt-ridden, isolated, and alone. (Bardos, Hercz, Friedenthal, Missmer, & Williams, 2015) No matter how much the doctor tried to reassure a mother, she always seemed to blame herself. In almost all miscarriages, mothers felt somehow responsible for why she could not keep the baby. She feels as if she did something wrong, searching her mind, thinking of all she could have done that may have prevented it from happening.

Before enduring the personal sting of miscarriage, I had only heard about it in passing. I gave it little thought. I had nothing to worry about because I already had one healthy pregnancy, and I was in good shape. I never thought it would happen to me. Before my son passed, I could not empathize with the depth of pain involved in such a loss.

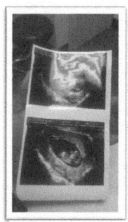

Figure 2 My sonogram taken a day before miscarriage

The emotional pain far surpassed the physical agony for me. Bodily harm is so much easier to heal - I was in and out of the hospital overnight but dealing with the grief takes longer to subside. Because of the emotional toll that miscarriage can take on a person, post-miscarriage care also includes counseling. The American Pregnancy Association reports that some women experience physical symptoms from their emotional distress. Issues such as fatigue, trouble sleeping, difficulty concentrating, loss of appetite, frequent episodes of crying, broken or suffering relationships with family or friends, self-harm, and suicidal thoughts or attempts. I had experienced every single one of these myriads of emotions almost immediately after the pregnancy loss. It was a dreadful rollercoaster, and an almagation that throw me into functional depression.

A single incident alone may not create a traumatic experience. However, when unfortunate events get compounded over time, it may time just one thing to causes internal injury. Consider the saying, "The straw that broke the camel's back." The worst part of the entire ordeal was the feeling that no one could see the depth of my pain. It was not just the grief from the pregnancy loss that was overtaking me, but years of feeling disrespected, dismissed, and ostracized. It all rolled into one, and I was slipping expeditiously in a dark place. Still, help came. Most often, the support came from places and people I least expected. I began to write more and meditate. I recommend every strategy in this book that incorporated to lift me from what was swiftly becoming an abyss.

The first lesson I had to learn was to forgive myself for everything I allowed to infiltrate my head and hurt. On the surface, I put up a strong front, but in the quietness of my home, I was a broken girl who could not stop the tears. I was grieving not just for my baby boy but the condition of my life. I was suffering in silence, so I had to learn how to be kind to myself. We often extend compassion to others but are the hardest on ourselves, especially in times of struggles. I needed to give myself room to heal and grow again without self-judgment or haste.

All those symptoms were a recipe for emotional trauma, and it was brewing. The hormonal changes from the miscarriage did not help, either. Everything became intensified but releasing the toxins from this unfortunate situation was part of my healing stages. I became adamant about adopting practices to move closer to happiness, and I became passionate about rising. I wanted change. My son's death, combined with my failed relationships, failed friendships, failed business ideas, and my cousin's death, were all compounded. It hurt, yet slowly with the right exercises, I began to believe that I was enough again with every waking day.

Courtney Lancaster was the Lead Special Education teacher in her department and a fantastic leader - a lady small in stature but significant in her presence. She was a patient leader and dealt with our students effectively with various disabilities, from Autism to emotional disturbance. On learning of her pregnancy loss, it surprised me because, despite her agony, Cortney continued to work with fidelity with a smile. She had a broken heart with the loss of over one miscarriage, but she did not show it. Below she shared how stress and pregnancy loss affected her life, and all she had to do to cut through the strings of grief.

> *My job has always been stressful because of the kind of person that I am. I make my job my life, and that is just how it is- no matter how hard I try to change. I was six days late but didn't think anything because of the stress associated with my job. Jokingly, my fiancé brought home a pregnancy test, and once the little pink + appeared, we knew our lives were about to change. We were so shocked but so excited! Two days later, I*

25

started spotting. So, we rush to the hospital, and after hours of waiting, we find out that we lost the baby at only six weeks. Only two days of knowing our little baby even existed — two days of excitement. During the two weeks following, I was placed on bed rest and could not seem to stop crying. Every day was spent alone, crying. That was all I knew to do to grieve the loss. I worried about how I would tell my family. Worried about how I would explain my absence to my students upon my return to work. Worried that maybe I had done something to cause such a huge loss. I grieved silently and for a long period of time. Miscarriages aren't typically something you discuss with anybody, and I didn't even want to discuss it with my fiancé... I didn't want to cause him any more pain.

Months pass by, and while the crying stopped, the grieving silently continued. Six months later, my fiancé and I were cleared to try again. We were so excited. The doctors said the last miscarriage was likely due to a category X medication that I was on prior, so there was no concern for any future pregnancies now that I have discontinued the medication. After two months of trying to conceive, the little pink + appeared on another pregnancy test, and this time we made it our mission to do everything right. I ate healthily, took my vitamins religiously, drank my recommended amount of water, exercised within my doctors' limits, and took absolutely no medication. After ten weeks, we were told our rate of miscarriage went down significantly, so we decided to tell our families. Our families were thrilled to have an addition to the family. Everyone was counting down to June 24, 2019. It was finally happening for us.

Two weeks later, I started bleeding while at work. This time, it was not spotting like I had experienced before. This was full on, uncontrollable bleeding. I finished out my workday, then drove to the emergency room to meet my mom and my fiancé. After hours of waiting, tests, and sonograms, the doctor walked in to tell us that we had lost the baby. The tests had shown that the baby died at eight weeks, but that my body did not realize it until right about 12 weeks. Twelve weeks of excitement only to end with the same result. This time was different, though. I had to have a procedure to remove the remains because I was too far along in the pregnancy to process the miscarriage without medical intervention. Again, I spent my

26

days crying, without much to say to anyone. I packed up all the things we purchased for our new baby and threw them in a closet where they could hide until the pain was gone. I started to hate the God that I had always believed. I started to think to myself, "Why would he do this to me time and time again? Why would he let me grow a baby to lose it weeks later?". I felt guilty and like I had to be the problem. What was so wrong with me that I could not carry a baby to full term? The guilt was consuming. The grief was consuming.

For months I envied other moms. I'm an educator, so I see all kinds of parents. When encountering the ones who did not seem to pay much attention to their children, I would think to myself how unfair it was for them to have several healthy babies. I would walk past the baby aisles at the store and cry a little. Even months later, people would ask me "How's the baby?" or "Is it a boy or a girl?". I would have to relive that trauma all over again to explain my loss.

Bottling up the anger, grief, guilt, and sorrow was not healthy for me. I knew that but talking about it was much more difficult. For a while, I thought if I didn't think or talk about the miscarriage, the pain would go away. This theory proved to be false, as it has almost been one full year since my first miscarriage, and I still am grieving. I grieve every day. I finally decided I was ignoring these feelings for far too long — this only prolonged the healing. So, I decided to start attending weekly counseling sessions to work through my emotions.

Through these sessions, I learned that talking and thinking about the miscarriage was the only way to work through the emotions of it. I have found a couple of friends who were willing to let me vent, and I finally opened up to my fiancé about how I was feeling. Once I let my feelings be known, everything started to get a little easier. My family, friends, and colleagues all started showing me grace in my day to day life. I also started leaning towards God again. Even though I was angry and didn't understand why my babies were taken from me, I remembered that I don't always need to know why. I needed to work through my emotions, get close to The Lord again, and to work on myself. So, that is exactly what I am doing. The anger is not gone by any means. I still think about the "what

27

ifs" and the grief every day. But every day, I also learn new ways to work through my grief. Every day I get a little stronger.

-   Courtney, 2019

We all respond to adversity in different ways. It is crucial to recognize when hurting to reduce ongoing suffering. No one else can dictate how an event affects you. Your experiences are personal. No one else can invalidate the legitimacy of your reactions to those situations. Do not compare your trauma to anyone else. Instead, take an inventory of your life and apply healing actions.

It is alright to admit you are

broken.

Losing my only son

Pregnancy loss is taboo. While it is a topic that many rarely share, it is common among more women than you may know. My story may not be the same as Cortney's or other women's, but we need healing just the same.

After a long day of work and yelling at students, I was sure I had raised my blood pressure to ridiculous levels. When I got home, I was so relieved to sit down. Like clockwork, heartburn kicked in, so I made tea as usual and sat back down, thinking nothing more of it. Then heartburn turned into a feeling of flatulence, but it would not pass. It felt stuck, so I kept drinking hot tea for release that did not come. Before long, the pain from what I thought was gas got worst and turned into crippling cramps. I folded over on all fours. The doctor on call after hours instructed me to take Tylenol and drink more water. She told me there was nothing to worry about unless I bled. Since there was no blood, I was less worried and prayed to my belly that my boy would stay put. But the pain escalated. It was so intense that it forced me to rush to the bathroom. I ran to the toilet, hoping that only waste would come out. Instead, it was my son. There, in the toilet's bowl, was his developing body, head, and beady eyes. He was gone.

I was alone, and the bleeding began. When the paramedics came, they tried in vain to distract me from the excruciating pain. By now, blood was everywhere. They checked my vitals, put me on the stretcher, and loaded me into the ambulance. The ride to the hospital was the longest drive of my life. As I grabbed hold of the paramedic's arm, tears welled up in my eyes at the thought I could die with nobody who loved me by my side. I did not want to leave my daughter, my existing child, the child motherless. Fear washed over me as the physical pain became even more overpowering.

29

This was trauma, and it was traumatic. I knew then that if I survived that I would have much work to do to heal. After continually expelling large clots in a constant pool of blood, the doctor informed me they

had to perform a Dilation and Curettage (D and C) surgery to stop the bleeding. I was in agony, so despite my initial objections, they convinced me it was the best thing to do. When I woke, the room was empty, and I laid there in complete stillness.

Figure 3, My daughter's drawing of my pregnant belly days before miscarriage

There was no one to comfort me. Although I was no longer scared, I was sad. I had never imagined that I would be in such a situation and had to go through by myself. Instead of crying, though, I began to write. Gratefully, my daughter was with her father, my ex-husband. Neither of them knew I was in the hospital, so the question haunted me on how I tell her I lost the sibling she had been long for and asking to have since she could speak. She was excited about the baby, even more than I was. Only days before, she was searching online for items to add to the baby's room. How could I tell her? She did not take it well. Her tears came flooding like a broken faucet, and my heart just broke all over again.

Pregnancy loss is painful. However, the lack of a support system can worsen your grief. It was in those days I conceptualized more of what it meant to become a woman. I was broken but not destroyed. I had another opportunity to live, embrace all the layers that each experience brings, and grow.

Cyber and Offline Bullying

A nam Tanoli was a model and fashion designer. She had a strong presence on social media with many followers. To them, she was an image of beauty with no care in the world. Her photos were always stylish, and she presented a happy demeanor to the world. Unbeknownst to everyone around her, she suffered from stress and depression. Viewers had been bullying her, but no one could tell that anything was wrong. In fact, from the video she posted before her death, she appeared resilient and sound. In that retaliatory video against online tormenters, she advised viewers, "Don't let it affect you, don't let it bring you down." There did not seem to be any visible signs it hurt her since she covered it quite well. Not even those closest to her knew of her suicidal thoughts. Anam was 26.

A person who seeks to harm or intimidate those they perceive as vulnerable is a bully, and they use technology as a weapon. Antagonizers are using the internet to spread venom. While this bullying trend is upsetting to adults, statistics blame cyberbullying for an increasing number of young people committing suicide. The internet allows bullies instant gratification available from social media. Cyberbullies are like traditional bullies except they have anonymity, hiding behind a screen and keyboards. It is unfortunate and preventable.

Online bullying includes threatening, humiliating, or intimidating information. When a person feels bombarded by negative remarks, there is a discouraging sense of self. It is much easier for these bullies to engage harmful behaviors because they believe their actions will go unpunished. (Pettalia, Levin, & Dickinson) Bullying, no matter whether it is traditional or cyber, causes significant emotional and psychological distress to victims. Anxiety, fear, depression, and low self-esteem are among symptoms of cyberbullying.

The best way to end cyberbullying is to turn off or disconnect the features that allow for these opportunities. However, many people find it hard to disconnect from social media or the negative information that is trending continuously. People must develop the discipline to cut ties from their electronic devices that funnel bad behaviors and gratify wrongdoers because the effects of bullying can play even on the victim's physical health. The stress of bullying can change eating habits and sleeping patterns, insomnia, nightmares, stomach ulcers, and skin conditions. (Gordon, 2018). Studies show that this may be due to the person's inability to disassociate from the bully's cruel behavior. Instead of disconnecting from the negativity, they internalize the bullies' behaviors, which causes deep-rooted problems.

While it is easy to assume that everyone is doing well from their online status, we must become conscientious that everyone is going through something we do not know. The widespread use of the internet has handed individuals with bad intentions an instrument to spew vengeance while masking themselves anonymously. It is a "faceless evil" and a growing threat for many, including teens, incapable of separating reality from their online personalities. Parents and loved ones must monitor their children's social media accounts and become more vigilant about recognizing the signs of depression. Looks can be deceiving, and we cannot always tell the pain behind someone's smile. We live in a world that thrives on immediate gratification combined with a need for constant external validation. The social media profile is just another way of camouflaging pain.

According to the Center for Disease Control and Prevention (CDC), suicide is the third leading cause of death among young people. For every single suicide killing, there are 100 self-slaughter attempts. Worst, victims of bullying are two to nine times more likely to commit this self-murder than those who were non-victims. Cyberbullying, however, is not only responsible for these deaths. The compounded effects of emotional trauma from sexual, physical, or other abuse are also culprits. Although we cannot prevent all self-harm, warning signs are indicating a need for help. Pay attention to signs of depression, giving away favorite possessions, expressing that they cannot handle things anymore, or making comments that things would be better without them. (Bullying and Suicide, n.d.)

While the internet is a powerful resource, we must remain mindful of the ongoing dangers, especially for the most vulnerable. Since a person can hide behind a keyboard, bullying online happens often without consequences, but it can leave an indelible mark on their victims. Bullying, whether done online or otherwise, causes significant and lasting distress.

Domestic Abuse

D omestic abuse is bullying that occurs more often than victims report, and it no one should take it lightly. It is a way for one person to establish their precedence while using demeaning methods and intimidation tactics to coerce the other person into compliance. As the name suggests, domestic abuse happens among people who live in the same home where they should feel the safest and most protected. It is a crime that leaves victims emotionally traumatized.

The term is also interchangeable with domestic violence, wife-beater, or intimate partner violence. According to the CDC, domestic abuse varies in frequency and severity. It can happen on a continuum that ranges from one episode to more constant attacks. No one can determine how many incidents will cause an impact on the victim. The behaviors of domestic abuse happen in different degrees. We can divide it into four main categories: physical, sexual, stalking, and psychological.

Physical violence is the easiest to detect because it involves hitting, kicking, or other types of physical force. It leaves a mark. Sexual abuse is physical violence, and happens one person forces the other person to have sex when they do not want to do so. It may also include attempting to force them to participate in a sex act, sexual touching, or a non-physical sexual event, such as sexting, when the person does not or cannot consent. The receiver of unsolicited nude photographs could consider the message as sexual abuse. (CDC - Injury - Intimate Partner Violence Consequences, n.d.)

Stalking usually takes place after a breakup or with some rejection. It is a conniving way to get a person's attention. Like domestic abuse, stalking triggers fear or causes your safety to be of concern. While stalkers can be strangers, often they are ex-lovers, family members, or someone who had shown an interest in dating you. Now, with the widespread use of technology and the internet, information is more accessible to stalkers. Abusers can locate those tried to get away by moving. They can even use identity theft and other means to access online and banking accounts that could leave you ashamed or in a financial bind.

National figures show that cyberstalking victims tend to be females during the college ages 18-29, but women are not the only targets. A survey of 765 students at Rutgers University and the University of Pennsylvania found 45% of stalkers to be female and 56% male. National figures show most stalkers to be male by overwhelming margins (87%). Men represented over 40% of stalking victims in the Penn-Rutgers study. (Moore, n.d.)

Cyberstalking is equally dangerous as traditional ways of stalking. It can bring physical harm, mental exhaustion, and emotional turmoil. It can also cause economic damage if they have access to your financial records, business, or investment properties. Draining someone's bank account, posting compromising images of a person, or sending unsolicited sexual photos are examples of cyberstalking. Situations that leave you feeling vulnerable, helpless, and destitute may have more adverse effects than the eyes can see.

We can consider verbal and nonverbal aggression as psychological abuse depending on the extent and frequency. At first, victims may not realize the intention until that running joke becomes more constant or that single comment slowly turns into a berating of your skills, appearance, or worth. While it may not be so obvious, it becomes clear that they intend to harm with increasing frequency. As

34

the receiver, you may question if you are overly sensitive. You may
blame yourself for not being enough for that person, or question why
you are allowing them to treat you with some animosity. However, the
abuser's sole goal is to have dominion over you. They want to establish
control over you. Since verbal or nonverbal abuse does not show
physical damage, people have underestimated the psychological
impact.

Domestic violence is a serious issue. It can cause significant health
issues or even fatality, yet people respond to it differently. Gender and
socio-economic status influence how people behave in a domestic
violence situation. According to the Federal Bureau of Investigation
(FBI), domestic violence is the leading cause of injury to women
between the ages of 15 to 44. While others most often perceive men as
perpetrators in abusive relationships, women are not always the
victims. The statistic shows that women are the most abusive towards
children, and there is an increased number of men who have reported
violence at women's hands. Francisco is a 54-year-old man who
suffered physical and verbal abuse from his mother, so he ran away at
11, becoming a Mexico City streets product. Determined to have a
better life, he worked hard to secure a job he loves and giving back to
the community. Despite the number of years that have passed and his
relative success, though, Francisco had not recovered from the trauma
caused by his mother, yet he wore the scars well.

Although living on the streets was hard, he admits that was the best
decision of his life. Looking back, he realized that his mother was
hurting. She was also a result of abuse and lovelessness. Hurting
people hurt people. "You could see it in her eyes," he said. "They were
always empty and cold." Francisco enjoys his life now but admits that
he is not fully healed from the terrible things his mother put him
through. "When a mother does not love you, there is no healing. There
is no cure for that." Worst, he felt broken after his mother pass
without uttering a word of apology to anyone - she did not appear
remorseful.

The reports of mothers who do awful things to their children or women who abuse their lovers may not be as common knowledge or as widespread as other abuses, but Francisco is not alone. Men and women alike are carrying emotional baggage and even physical scars from an abusive mother. When the woman who should love you the most treats you like she does not, it is painful and can cause deep-rooted issues. The symptoms of which may include low self-esteem and looking for love in the wrong places. There is a void and ache as you try to figure out why she did not care for you. Still, healing is necessary. It is hard work, long, painful, ongoing process, but healing is possible. Since there is a complex perception of men involving pain and feelings, few communities establish facilities that caters to the physical violence or emotional trauma that men experience. Our society has a construct an idea that men do not hurt, yet if they do, they must "man up." This faulty reasoning is dangerous because it continues a perplexing trend of toxic tendencies. This trend must end. Pain and healing are not gender-bias. Our societal norms, expectations, and traditions must shift to address the growing number of men who need help.

Sexual Assault

Childhood trauma happens through various situations, such as divorce, death, illness, bullying, to name a few. The effect of childhood trauma is long-lasting, and unresolved childhood trauma can leave a person feeling vulnerable, insecure, fearful, and helpless. These tendencies need proper attention to heal. When you read the stories of people now in their 30s, 40s, and 50s recalling molestation and raped starting as early as a baby, you sympathize with their brokenness. Unfortunately, mothers have put their children in harm's way and fathers have neglected to protect them. Too many doubted children who spoke out. They have even shunned or blamed them when they share how someone had molested them.

Research shows that children know the person who exploited them. Although sexual assault among family members is a well-kept secret, its

36

effects always manifest. Many have swept this crime under the carpet, leaving innocent children torn, confused, abandoned only to grow up to become dysfunctional adults exhibiting signs of Post-Traumatic Stress Disorder (PTSD). Even more tragic, some victims of sexual abuse become predators themselves, preying on innocence.

Whitney McCain is an inspiring writer and author. We met through our interactions on social media. One day, she shared her experience with a sexual deviant, her maternal grandfather. She explained that the years of rape left her life entangled with feelings of shame, rejection, and abandonment. For a time, she battled with drug addiction and remaining in physically abusive relationships. The most heart-wrenching part of the story was when she shared that her abuser asked for her forgiveness on his deathbed. For some, this is an all too familiar tale. The story of a trusted person who defiled a child intimately. All sexual assaults are painful. However, when it is a family member, that can be an even harder pill to swallow. Situations such as this are the beginning of trauma, which may leave a scar on somebody's heart. Unfortunately, while there are some things we would rather block out from our past, childhood traumas are not always short-lived.

Whitney describes that awful day. After her parents went to work, her grandfather sent her sister to the store then called her into his bedroom. She had no reason to suspect foul play because she trusted him. As soon as she entered the room, he raped her. When she summoned the courage to tell her mother, her mother did not believe her, so the abuse continued for years. Whitney survived, but she was left scarred for life. It affected her relationships, including the one with her mother, and her mental health. When her mother called her to the hospital to say her final goodbyes, she was angry. Distraught, she went there, sat by his bedside, held his hands, and told him that she forgave him. Whitney had learned a valuable lesson - acknowledging and releasing those who had hurt you brings personal healing. The forgiveness was not only to release him or to set his soul free, but it was for her to experience the freedom she needed to live a healthy life.

Whitney's mother did not believe her, and her father was not there to protect her from the onslaught of her grandfather. As she felt that no one came to her rescue, the anxiety level involved in this situation was exhausting, and it wore on her sense of self. She blamed herself when nothing else can make sense. Without releasing this traumatic event, Whitney would have continued to live a life of destruction.
Sexual deviance is not gender-specific. Women can exploit children. I once interviewed a guy who shared the story of his 18-year-old babysitter who sexually assaulted him when he was only five. Men have a different view of sexual assault than women do. I overheard a 27-year-old father of two girls boasting he was 15 years old dating 50-year-olds with his mother's permission. His mother encouraged those relationships, and he grew up in a pedophile-friendly environment where his direct family accepted these inappropriate tendencies.

Self-care is taking time out to address what makes you feel heavy and assisting in releasing burdensome emotions. Think about when someone does something to put you in a foul mood, which ruins your entire day because it consumes your thoughts. Untreated emotions can render us ineffective and cause us to miss out on enjoying life. Therefore, we must include practical strategies to release the negative association from our hearts.

Everything that happened before now is past – it is gone and not something we can ever get back. We have experienced glorious highs, but some know the rock bottom lows. With every memory, we can recreate pieces of those moments. Our lingering feelings towards those events help us assess if the situation was positive, negative, or traumatic. We seldom want to things, so we must become mindful of detaching our emotions from the past pains. Consider the lessons learned but do not hold yourself a prisoner to yesterday. In every chance you get, permit yourself to feel the freedom you deserve.

Liberate yourself from the judgment of others and manage the negative self-talk that may come from your head. Despite what you know, everyone has experienced something they do not want to share with you. Their pain is just as valid as yours. Everyday people are dealiong with a hurt that none of us can see, so be nice. Also, remember to not put anyone on a pedestal. No one should hold the power to destroy you emotionally with their opinion. Learn yourself, and being to live your truth.

Heal and grown through it.

Time alone does not make it better. You must give time something to work with for better to come.

After experiencing a traumatic situation, learn to be kind to yourself; show compassion. Sometimes, we are our worst critics. It is more natural for us to help others during difficulties, but we are the harshest with ourselves. To experience true healing, we must learn to see ourselves through new eyes. You are worthy of love and deserve forgiveness. Like others, you should have a second chance. Do not hold yourself hostage, to the perils of the past.

In a study comparing college student's retrospective self-reports of fear, shame, guilt, anger, and sadness among four types of traumatic events (sexual assault, physical assault, transportation accidents, and illness/injury), those in the sexual assault group reported higher levels of post-trauma emotion than the other trauma type groups. (Amstadter & Vernon, 2008)

When someone feels threatened, they may regress to a time they felt the most protected. Others blame themselves for the incident, which may present itself in varying degrees from helplessness to sleeping disorders. People who have suffered from several stressful situations develop tendencies that keep them operating in survival mode. They may abuse sex or drugs, become abusive towards others, harm themselves, or participate in attention-seeking behaviors. Although these habits are coping mechanisms, they are sabotaging their chances for true happiness.

English teachers ask students to write essays or personal narratives to assess their writing skills. During this time, we discover more meaningful information about students, too. This time, we asked them to reflect on a time that has the most impact on their lives. My senior class shared what was the most traumatic situation to date for them. From their writing samples, you could see how circumstances that may have been overlooked by others left a mark on them.

Student A was a brilliant student, intelligent, assertive, reliable, and leading naturally. She was a self-advocate. It took time and patience to help her realize that I was not against her. From the moment she came into my classroom, she looked ready to fight. She was always

41

defensive. It was not until she could take charge of a class project that her attitude began to shift. Her anecdotal note explained her mood swings and overall demeanor.

Although she was an extrovert, she was also functionally depressed, affecting her relationships with others. After writing this note, she learned that our classroom was a safe space, and she became more relaxed than she ever had been with us. She complained less about pains, was present more often, and was overall more pleasant. Student A was even less defensive by the end of the school year.

Part of our healing is contingent upon who is surrounding us. There is a saying: We are the five people who hang out with the most, meaning if those people add to your insecurity, you will never heal. However, if they nurture an environment of love, tolerance, and trust, you are more likely to grow and thrive.

An unforgettable time in my life was when I moved to Texas. I did not want to move here. I was going to be far away from my family, and I used to be friends. I was going to miss everything. I moved to Texas on August 23, 2017 and have been here ever since. This move was so hard. I was depressed for months. My depression was so deep to the point where I would lie about being sick so that I could stay home from school. I traveled so much to St. Louis because I really missed my family. I have even though about moving back, but that would mean not seeing my mommy and brother all the time. I would travel to see them all the time. I hope I can finally convince my mom to get an iPhone so that we can Facetime each other all the time. My moving back to St. Louis will help me improve my independence, show my mom that I am able to do things on my own. I miss getting out the house and going places with my friends. Since I have been here, I stay in the house, in my room listening to music in a bad mood. This move will never be unforgettable.

Student B was equally feisty. She had moved from New York, of Puerto Rican and Black parents, and with many personalities. Although I have had taught her two different years, there were days where she reacted as if we were meeting for the first time.

When she first came to our school, she made friends, but it was quiet. Soon after, I learned that she was shy and had no hesitation about being assertive. She was not a defiant student, per se, but she had room to manage her emotions so that her attitude would not get her into hot water. After writing about her most memorable moment, her temperament seemed more settled. We laughed more together, and she seemed more interested in the class' activities. Her anecdote put things in perspective for me. Every situation has a different significance for a person, and what may not be meaningful to one person may cripple another. Her note highlighted the value of a father's role in children's self-identity and confidence.

> *My mom and dad dated for a long time before they had my two big brothers, Axel and Joune. Three years later, they had me. I was the youngest. My brothers got to meet him, but I never did. I remember my family always talking about him. When I was six, I remembered his name. As a little girl, I remember feeling mad all the time. Then, when I was ten, he showed up outside of our house. I saw him and felt nothing. No happiness. No nothing. He said to me, "I am your dad," to which I screamed, "No. You are not! You will never be my dad. You do not love me, my mom, nor this family. If you did, you would never have left." So, I never had a dad. He came around a few times, but he always told me that I would never be anything in life. He admitted that he did not love my mother or me. He even claimed that I was not his child because I was too light-skinned, and all his other children are black. That made me feel terrible! Although I heard the judge telling him later that I was his child, it did not matter. He does not care. He never loved me, and I think that is why I have trust issues today.*

Quick Write:

Although childhood should be a period of innocence, naivety, and pure bliss, some of us were robbed of that light early on. Overwhelming occurrences in our early years could drastically affect how we behave or respond to situations as adults with people abusing sex or drugs to cope with the pain. Unfortunately, no matter how desperately we may conceal these dismal events, the unresolved issues find a way to manifest itself in our behaviors.

Think back to your earliest memories. What is one event that you recalled that caused you the most pain? You will go into more details about this in the final chapter.

_____

_____

_____

_____

_____

_____

_____

_____

_____

_____

_____

III.   Symptoms of Emotional Trauma

Trauma is not a disorder. The etymology of the word trauma goes back to the Greek word for a wound. When physical injury exceeds the body's capacity for repair, there may be lasting damage or death. We can say the same for emotional trauma. In our fast-paced world, with stresses and strains, emotional trauma like others is almost ubiquitous. The significant difference between physical difference and one that is more psychological lies in our fallible minds. (Kirmayer, Lemelson, & Barad, 2007)

Our minds and body respond to horrors in diverse ways, and no one can predict how anyone will respond. When I was about nine, I witness a man getting ran over by a lorry. I watched as his entire head got crushed from the weight of this vehicle, but interestingly I had no recollection of this event until writing this book. The memory was there but locked away to protect me from any possible psychological harm because of its horrific nature. Another person may have had a complete adverse reaction to that scene that may show more obvious signs of distress.

One of my students explained how her grandfather's death traumatized her. Although the incident happened when she was much younger, as a senior in high school, she was still learning how to cope with his absence. The response to trauma, emotional or otherwise, has different faces. According to (Emotional and Psychological Trauma, n.d.), the symptoms of emotional and psychological injuries are diverse, ranging from shock, irritability, mood swings to anger, self-blame, and hopelessness. Suicide is of increasing concern as more children, teenagers, and men are taking their own lives. When we recollect the old traumas, we should also remember that we can change nothing already passed. It has happened, and life must move on. How we heal determines the quality of our journey.

Creating a Monster

When you meet a 16-year-old full of rage and behaving recklessly, you know that she did not get there on her own. Her environment created her. As a teacher in the 21st century, classroom management is essential. No lesson planning will supersede your ability to manage the various personality and learning abilities in one room. As an administrative intern on the high school campus, you meet all the students with behavior issues. There is a link between many of them who had difficulty following the student code of conduct. They are angry. As you know, hurting people seek to act out. They want their pain to be acknowledged even if no one renders treatment.

Camille was one of those students. She was persistently insubordinate, a consistent classroom disruption with no regard for anyone else. A day after returning from suspension, someone called her down to the principal's office in response to a similar referral about her behavior. When she arrived, she was immediately irritated. As she heard the consequences of her actions, she became increasingly aggravated, the volume in her voice increased, and she threw things around the room. She was out of control. In her manic state, she screamed, "That is why students shoot up the school. Forget the warnings." Her parent had to take her home. A few weeks later, her mother called the police, on they arrested her for grievous bodily assault.

There is an underlying stew of unaddressed emotional issues for many students who act out in this way. In Camille's case, she experienced emotional trauma from her mother, who had left her when she was six years old. Her father and grandmother raised her in a different state. One night, her mother showed up and took her without warning. When she found out that her father and grandmother allowed her mother to do it, she was livid. Among other things, Camille felt a sense of abandonment. Although she attended therapy sessions, she was always in a volatile state and ready to explode at any moment. She could not let it go.

46

Given the same situation, not all children would behave in the same way. Again, people react to trauma in different. Parents must become more mindful of the emotional damage caused by their decisions and do their best to address the issues. When they cannot deal with the repercussions alone, they must solicit the assistance of skilled professionals. Everyone's ability to let go of the past will improve their chances of healing from emotional trauma.

PTSD

The research defines Post Traumatic Stress Disorder (PTSD) as a mental health condition or anxiety disorder that develops following a traumatic event, which can be a lifelong diagnosis. PTSD affects over three million people per year in the United States. Not every dangerous or shocking situation results in post-traumatic stress disorder. According to medical scientists, PTSD occurs when a person is incapable of recovering from the trauma symptoms on their own. They exhibit behaviors consistent with intense fear, helplessness, and stress that affects their function in their everyday life. Treatments for this disorder include a combination of pharmaceutical drugs and alternative medicines.

Peter was my friend. He was forever jovial and seemed to not have a care in the world. His thin frame was unintimidating, but his personality was rock solid. He came across as the guy you take home to your parents - an overall nice guy. He would share stories of his time in the military. A few times, they were a little grim, but he never lingered on the tales or elaborated on the details. I could see that there was something more there.

One day, I asked him. He hesitated but admitted that he had had PTSD. As I listened to him, I recall my time on the military base as another wife shared stories about her "crazy" husband who had just returned from Iraq. He was not allowed around the children because he almost shot one. Peter's story would give new meaning to the saying, "You cannot judge a book by its cover." He was a troubled man who pretended well as he tried to regain some control of normalcy.

I was first deployed in 2007 to Iraq. My first friend who was killed died a month later. His vehicle was hit with an IED, killing him and severely wounding 8 others in the process. This was their first mission outside the wire. This was when I knew our deployment would be terrible. My first-time seeing death over there was different than I expected. It was on the base. A local Iraqi had hung himself after he got word his family had been executed. My friend discovered the body in a sheet metal structure, hanging by a set of stairs, motionless. I remember thinking one of his eyes looked funny and that it wasn't so bad. The next time was more what I thought I would see. I stepped in the remains of an Iraqi man who attempted to disarm a roadside bomb and it went off. He was everywhere. A week later, a suicide bomber who detonated too early had his head fused to his hip bone and I remember thinking, "that is strange." His face was swollen, almost like a balloon, no eyes. No teeth. Morbid curiosity was my strongest feeling. Remembering my friend's death started to feel worse by month 2. I was attacked on Easter Sunday, 2008. Massive IED. I was knocked unconscious and woke up inside the vehicle. I had previously been on the machine gun up top. Ended up with a traumatic brain injury from the blast. I remember crying later that day, but I don't remember much else.
The Siege of Sadr City... 2008.

We were shot at daily. Attacked often. We killed and watched people die. But my first taste of mental trauma came from me shooting someone I thought was trying to shoot me. I heard a bullet fly past my head. Very, very close. This wasn't in a firefight. This was while I was pulling guard outside of a building. Sniper. He missed. The Soldier behind me told me to get down. I didn't. I spun around and shot him. Twice. Killing him.

I remained silent. He didn't have a gun. He was just running. He wasn't the shooter.
I never reported the killing or the shot. Some heard me return fire, obviously, but I said I thought I was shot at, so I fired in the direction of the shot to hopefully get them to run. I was scolded by my squad leader.

150 meters away, there was a body. Someone had moved it by the next morning.
He was someone's dad, brother, son...

THAT was my first taste of misery. It replays often.
After that, the violent things added up. Every death was just a little more weight added on to my shoulders. Every kill was questioned by a trial in my head. I returned home from that deployment and turned to alcohol and mindless sex. I'd sleep 3 hours a night getting drunk and laid. I'd ignore my friends. They were very concerned. But that was what I felt I needed.

I deployed to Iraq again in 2010. This time for only a year. And in 2012, I was in Afghanistan.
At some point in every year, from 2007-2013, I was in either Iraq or Afghanistan. The stories I have are too many to count. I've seen an infant that was executed in the middle of the street. I've seen women's bodies shot and behead, left out in the sun to rot. I used to dream about being those men who could do such horrible things. I remember running to a counselor after waking up from a nightmare where I was having sex with a woman, consensually, then I blindfolded her and slowly shoved a filet knife through her eye and into her brain... as I was having sex with her. This was too much for me. I needed help.

I've put my own gun in my mouth. I've had many problems dealing with my nightmares. I can't handle failing at personal relationships because I feel as though I need someone to love me to prove I'm sane.
I've seen doctors and counselors. I've been to group therapy. Nothing seems to work. The problem I have is being intelligent enough to know their tricks. To know what they are trying to do to make me feel better. I had one doctor tell me to look into the mirror and tell myself I am a good person 20 times every morning. I told her to get fucked.

Now, I'm better. I haven't had a panic attack in almost 2 years! I stick to the present as best I can. I have a beautiful wife and child. If I have a nightmare, I touch my wife, cuddle her if it's extremely rough. If I have some disturbing flashbacks, I look at my daughter. She's beautiful and almost always smiling. I keep their pictures close.

49

Love keeps me sane. Having someone who loves me proves that I'm not hopeless. She had a child with me... I'm a father. I have a purpose and I am loved. I'm not lying to a mirror 20 times. It's real. That's what it took. That scary part? I'd let anyone love me like that and latch onto them. I just hope I'm not using her as a crutch. THAT are what scares me now.

Peter revealed to me that behind every smile hides a pain so deep that only love can heal. Everybody struggles with something we do not know about so we cannot rely on a smiley face or an upbeat attitude to confirm that they are doing all right. While I was familiar with incidents that may occur in combat, it was difficult to know that someone you cared about had experienced such vivid and cruel conflicts.

During our conversation, I asked if he had forgiven himself. "No," he said. "I don't think I ever will. I look at my morality and know what is right and wrong. I have always known. I cannot forgive myself for my actions. I believe it is selfish. I believe I should be punished for the bad things I have done." While he blames himself, he wants to become a better person. Daily, he walks on a path towards recovery and releasing the guilt to help him heal from the emotional traumas.

Peter's confession about love is empowering. He has a renewed sense of purpose, and it is helping him through the disorder. Still, I could not help but notice that of all the things he had experienced in combat, his number one fear today was using his wife as an emotional crutch. "Love keeps me sane. Having someone who loves me proves I'm not hopeless. She had a child with me. I'm a father. I have a purpose, and I am loved. I'm not lying to a mirror 20 times. It's real. That's what it took. That scary part? I'd let anyone love me like that and latch onto them. I just hope I'm not using her as a crutch. That is what scares me now."

We are not always the innocent party in situations that cause pain. From Peter's story, the one who inflicts pain is not exempt from the pain itself. Even when we are the culprit in any situation, our heart yearns for love and acceptance. Like Peter, too many believe that they do not deserve happiness, so they participate in activities that bring pain to gratify their guilt. You do not have to be in a war zone to experience PTSD. Camille's inability to deal with the problems inside of her heart and head created PTSD. To live and love, we must learn how to forgive ourselves. It may be hard to forgive ourselves because we feel that punishment will appease our guilt; it will not. Acknowledging the wrongdoing, taking strides to wellness, and letting go of the pain are steps towards healing.

Chapter Summary/Key Takeaways

In this chapter, we defined emotional trauma and gave examples of how a situation can have a lasting impact on people, including small children. We learned that no one could dictate to another person what becomes traumatic despite the magnitude of the circumstances. Unless healing occurs, hurting people will continue to hurt other people.

In the next chapter, we will dive into strategies for assisting in our healing from emotional traumas.

Releasing Emotional Trauma

In 2011, an Ohioan woman who recently moved to Texas, was unqualified for food stamp benefits, apparently due to a lack of enough documentation. One day, she walked into the welfare office with her 10-year-old son and 11-year-old daughter and was again unable to receive benefits. Things turned grim as she pulled out a gun and turned it on her children, then killed herself.

Emotional trauma creates psychological and other problems that are not always visible. The outcome of those unresolved issues, however, can be deadly. To heal from mental trauma takes a plethora of resources and strategies. For some, it is as simple as letting go of unpleasant feelings, but for others, it means medication and therapy. The end goal in releasing emotional heavyweights is to handle memories that you have long been avoiding, discharge pent-up "fight-or-flight" energy that will help us learn to regulate our emotions and rebuild the ability to trust again. While everyone may not need a professional, a specialist is a valuable resource. It may use different therapy approaches to release the thoughts that are causing your ongoing pain resulting in a host of unfortunate events.

Kevin struggled in school. Later, the psychologists diagnosed him with a learning disability. In class, he was selective about whom he spoke to but was still sociable. He was an aspiring musician and had a YouTube channel showcasing his skills. Even still, there was something dark about him. The days when he came into class with a heavy mood, he would say nothing and just put his head down on the desk. Some days the stench of marijuana was all over him. It also became clear that whenever school would break for an extended holiday, he would get distraught. The school counselor got involved in assessing what was troubling him.

One day, he was in the counselor's office and was not looking good. As I walked into the room, I could sense the heaviness. He was not ok at all. Instead of asking him what was going on, I just hugged him. He was a child in my arms. He cried and cried. Whatever it was, it was tormenting him. He shared that the voices in his head were telling him to kill his mother. It was not the first time, either. He was seeing spirits and played with an Ouija board. Under the counselor's guidance and his mother's permission, they directed him to medical professionals to receive additional aid. Kevin had experienced some traumatizing events at an early age and was consumed by it all. He could not forgive. He would not let it go, and the memories continued to haunt him.

Just like Alcoholics Anonymous, the first step towards emotional recovery is accepting that there is a problem. Acknowledging that you are hurting, that something is wrong, or that there must be a change is a necessary stage of healing. You cannot start progress without doing something different. Proper recovery means no pretense. You cannot fake it until you make it with this one. You must go through the stages without trying to avoid the pain. Some days you will cry, but you cannot stay there. Some days you will be mad, but you cannot remain there. Although there will be times you force yourself to smile when you want to frown, that is not faking it. That is moving through the process and putting in the work for your change. Transformation happens when you do what is best though it is uncomfortable.

Release and Let Go

The longer we live, the more we learn none of us are exempt from hurt or disappointments. The more tools you have in your arsenal, the more equipped you will be to approach the different situations that will come up, helping to build resilience so that there is no longer a fear of being vulnerable.

Before my pregnancy loss, I was already on a personal journey to uncover hidden truths about myself. I have always been a reflective person, but I began to recognize an unfavorable cycle with age and experience I was determined to break the pattern. My intimate relationship was toxic. The relationship with my close friends was in turmoil. Overall, I had sense of complete disarray. I have a terrible habit of internalizing my hurt. Instead of acting out or getting angry at the other person, I wasted time scrutinizing myself, trying to figure out what I could have done to make a person treat me better. I spent a tremendous amount of time thinking about what other people thought of me in the past. It was all so stifling, and I wanted to change.

As a resilient and resourceful person, I intended to reconnect with the most authentic parts of me and build upon my strengths. I wanted to regain balance from all the life events that had thrown me out of whack. First, I made a conscious decision to release the memories I was holding on to for dear life and let go of the pain, the disappoints, and the abandonment that kept me hostage.

These seemingly insignificant activities made an impact in my stride towards healing from emotional entrapment:

Stop being afraid of my tears. I cried when I needed to and bawled when I had to, and it did not make me weak or complaining.

Journal Writing. It provided a release as I scribed my memories and allowed me a way to assess the severity of the events.

Affirmations. I wrote affirmations and placed them in places that I could see. Seeing positive words promotes positive self-talk. It is a powerful reminder.

Worked out often. The physical activity allowed me to release pent up negative energy, especially when it involved kicking or punching.

Drank plenty of hot tea. I love the warmth it brings me. It is comforting, so more is more. Caffeine-free.

Spent quality time with my daughter. Often, I am so distracted by life. I am there but not there. I was more purposeful with the time I spent with her.

Prayed. I prayed in the morning, at my desk at work, during my workout, as I drove, wherever it did not matter. It is a secret communication that grants me special help.

Meditated. I was so glad I incorporated this practice into my routine. Meditation, by far has brought me the most peace. It has allowed me the calm my thoughts while preparing for my day.

Got up. Although this sounds so simple, some days, getting out of bed was one of the hardest things to do. Getting up is a massive part of any victory.

Helped others. Giving back to others became part of my healing. We are all going through something, and some days I am the strong. Other days it is helping them that gives me the strength to carry on.

Nowadays, I rarely talk about my spiritual practices. However, in the process of self-rediscovery, I embraced the philosophy known as Omnism. The belief is that there is no one religion with all the truth, but all religions lead to the truth. It accepts that all religions have beneficial spiritual practices. My most recent life events forced me to a place of reckoning. It was painful and awkward, but I did not want to avoid it.

Once a Christian, I am familiar with fasting, praying, praise, and worship. During this time of my life, I had the strong urge to cry out to the Powers for help. I recited the Lord's Prayer, I sang, I meditated.

It took everything I knew to get me out of the dark place. I watched uplifting videos, listened to motivational speakers, and listened to high vibrational melodies to renew my mind. Music has a way of awakening your soul.

As I read the fundamental principles of Buddhism, I became comforted because I was not alone. Suffering is universal. We will all experience it, yet it has a purpose that brings about the end of our pain. Suffering and desires were at the root of all suffering. For me, this was true. My early childhood trauma and my own dismantled family left a strong urge for a healthy reciprocal relationship. I longed to meet the person who was the yin to my yang, but time and time again met representatives, not the real deal.

Since I had adapted to the Law of Attraction principle, we get what we think about the most, and we attract who we are into our lives, I had to look at myself. Was I the person I said I wanted, or was I, too, a forgery? While I seem to be on a loop of unfortunate circumstances, I was familiar with dealing with disappointments. This time, though, I wanted to change so much that I was willing to pay the price for my freedom. I had questioned myself too often. Thoughts of not being good enough plagued me. I questioned if I was good enough to be loved, and I wondered how much more perfect I had to become to get it. It was exhausting because the people who came into my life was far from flawless. They were broken individuals, and I was their rehabilitation center even though I needed healing myself. I spent many nights crying. Crying for what I wish I had and sobbing for what I wanted to have. I was still grieving for my loss and bellowing because I did not understand what else I needed to do to get what I desired. I had found the root of much of my anguish.

As a teacher, I have observed how mental and emotional anguish interferes with student progress and became increasingly aware of how many issues were rooted in unresolved trauma. One student sent a message asking, "How would you feel if I was dead?" Another showed up to school high, with marijuana in his pocket. Then, yet another declared that voices in his head are telling him to kill his mother. It became crystal clear we are people living in a cesspool of unresolved issues, and we must do whatever it takes to clean it up.

Quick Illustration: Read Priscilla's admission below. Think back to a time when you felt the most vulnerable? Below, draw a picture expressing what you felt like back then.

When I was six years old, a man who was a family friend sexually assaulted me. I kept quiet about it as most victims do. My grandmother saw everything and covered it up because the abuser was her husband. Unfortunately, neither of my parents notice, so I suffered alone, emotionally, even spiritually. I spent most of my childhood trying to hide behind the agony and ugliness of my experience. I asked myself, "How could they not know? Why did they not protect me?"

Self-Help Interventions

"Begin to think of yourself as being made of pure energy. I cannot emphasize enough how much damaged trapped emotions can do. Remember that they can affect you physically, emotionally, and mentally. They are made of pure energy, but they are negative energy, and the sooner you get rid of them, the better off you will be." Dr. Bradley Nelson

Studies show that releasing negative emotions can cause a reversal of physical ailments, such as high blood pressure or stress symptoms. It is also important to understand that cultivating positive emotions with the right practices can help achieve improved well-being over time and not just in the short term.

Emotion is a strong feeling deriving from one's circumstances, mood, or relationships with others, which are responses to significant changes within or around us. When someone experiences an emotional trauma, our body and mind trigger a response to adapt to our environment. If a negative emotion such as terror or anxiety becomes trapped in our bodies or get stuck on replay in our minds, it becomes toxic to our overall sense of self. Ultimately, healing from emotional trauma takes intentional, purposeful effort. We cannot rely on time alone to do it for us, and avoidance does not help. Healing is a process with no shortcuts. For the rest of this book, we will explore self-help options, such as counseling, meditation, journal writing, and music therapy, to get you on your path to recovery. However, if your symptoms persist or become worst, please consult a professional.

Counseling

When a person feels overwhelmed with grief or the shock from a traumatic event, it may be necessary to seek professional guidance. A licensed psychotherapist aims to help people cope with their physical, emotional, social, spiritual, and cognitive responses to trauma. They can help to assist emotional management or release feelings such as anxiety, rage, loneliness, and guilt. Even as a retrospective person with an ongoing understanding of yourself, there may come a time where having a professional to help you navigate and classify your experiences may be the best thing to do. Some therapists use regressive therapy to help clients realize past events that interfere with their current mental and emotional wellness.

In writing this book and testing the true nature of counseling, I started to ask myself some hard questions. For years, I had held on to the image of a frightened six-year-old me being forced behind furniture by a grown man. That was one recurring nightmare I continued to suppress for years, but after my first session with my counselor, I realized that the trauma started much earlier than that.

I was two years old. My mother had left me unattended in the bathtub filled with water. I almost drowned. I had completely forgotten this memory until that day. Although my mind had no recollection of my near-death experience, my emotions did not. It was traumatic, yet somehow, my mind and body did what it had to do to keep me going. Even though I did not remember, a sense of abandonment, neglect, and loneliness locked themselves into my subconscious, which may have contributed to the relationship dynamics between my mother and me.

"Do you have an example of true love in your life?"
"With who in your life do you feel like you can be 100% yourself?

As I sat in the counselor's office, sure of myself yet even more confident that I needed help, his two questions filled my head. Silence fell. I kept thinking and thinking of the best way to respond, but no answer came. There was no one that I could identify who exemplified love without conditions. From my experiences, I reasoned that I had to be damn near perfect to experience unconditional loved. People like the idea of me. I am confident, resourceful, and resilient, but I also understood that it was hard for them to accept me fully - flaws, insecurities, and all. In my reality, I was known by many but surrounded by very few.

As I pondered over these two questions, *"Do you have an example of true love in your life?" "With who in your life do you feel like you can be 100% yourself?,*, I was hard-pressed to find someone I felt I could truly be my authentic self without inhibitions.

The more I reflected on my relationships, the more there was an intrinsic tug to look back at my parents' relationships. Despite doing well in school and being grounded in church, childhood was a struggle for me. Life with my mother was challenging, and my dad's physical absence made me feel vulnerable. As I grew up and lived with my father, I would never have admitted it, but I was angry at him, too. While they have been doing the best they could have, I felt abandoned and never quite felt like I belonged.

After my session with the counselor, I pondered on those two questions. From all the things we talked about, those inquiries resonated with me the most. That is the purpose of counseling, to help you answer the right questions to get to the root of the problem and generate solutions. The answers may not come on the same day. Be patient. Today, I have a much better understanding of how events in my early childhood connect with my feelings of abandonment and a perpetual sense of loneliness. Internally, I battled to have validation from others. Their recognition and acceptance would mean I worthy of love.

Counseling combined with the therapy of writing this book allowed me to process my internal conflicts. Many times in my development journey, I believed I had overcome my childhood issues and resolved all the pain

61

associated with them, but as life happened, I found that there was more healing to do. The emotional trauma was still there. However, choosing to address this subject meant being mindful of my role as a writer and became even more conscious of my responsibility in my personal growth - my healing. Coincidentally, studies show that writing a memoir, especially concerning suffering and trauma, is a proven means of healing psychologically. (Painter, 2009) We will discuss this in more detail later. Life happens. Painful situations happen to us all. None of us can escape it. My reason for attending counseling was to receive clarity from an unbiased person. I wanted a professional who could help me navigate through unpleasant encounters so I would be better able to resolves obstinate conflicts and restore a deeper understanding of myself.

Finding the right counselor or therapist for you may take time to recover. Use all your resources to find your best fit. Ask your insurance company, family, friends, and even your professional network for referrals. If you go through your insurance company, they typically give you a few free sessions to "try out" the counselor. You also can speak to a counselor over the phone, instead of face to face, if that helps you be more comfortable.

Forgiveness

Forgiveness is the intentional and voluntary process by you change your feelings and attitude regarding an offense. By forgiving, a victim lets go of negative emotions, such as vengefulness. They may choose to reject recompense from or punishment of the offender, however legally or morally justified it might be. Forgiveness allows you an increased ability to wish the offender well. Forgiveness differs from condoning, excusing, forgetting, pardoning, and reconciliation. (Forgiveness, n.d.) If something still hurts you, pay attention. Emotionally pain is a sign that something is wrong. To ignore that pain means you are not healing. Healing means taking notice of the pain and addressing it. It does not mean ignoring it or pretending you feel nothing when you do. Forgiving the offender facilitiates your healing and brings peace. Whether you seek help from a professional or not, one step to recovery includes forgiveness – others and yourself.

Studies indicate that people who forgive are happier and live a much healthier life than those who carry the resentments from someone doing them wrong regardless of justifiable for them to do so. One study showed how forgiveness improves physical health. Moreover, in their discovery, they found that even when people thought about forgiving their offender, it led to more improved functioning in their cardiovascular and nervous systems. A study at the University of Wisconsin found the more forgiving people were, the less they suffered from a wide range of illnesses. On the other hand, less forgiving people reported a higher number of health problems. (Forgiveness, n.d.)

As research shows, although this may be a complicated process, it comes with astounding results. I had to learn how to release the pent-up anger about issues that stemmed from my childhood, the bitterness from feeling betrayed and abandoned, even the onset of self-hate sometimes became only possible when I forgave me first and the offenders second. It was a painful start which involved lots of tears, but once I got going, it got easier.

Even though there are situations where you were an innocent bystander, there are times where you must look around and recognize your contribution to the mess. Amid my crying, I had realized that I had to forgive myself for making the choices I made from hurt and self-doubt and forgive those who caused me harm when I did nothing to injure them. Forgiving those people gave me freedom, even though they were undeserving. Besides, it allowed me to set aside some of my baggage that would have forced someone else to pay for another person's mistakes. Now, you can release someone and never be in their company again; however, when you forgive yourself, you must learn how to treat yourself well - be kind to yourself.

One of the first tips a counselor gave me was to show myself compassion. I had just lost my son, and I was in a rush to get over it because I felt others expected that of me. I knew how to be nice to others when needed, yet it was not always the same story for me.

Prayer

Prayer to someone religious could mean a solemn request for help or expression of thanks addressed to God while it may only mean an earnest hope or wish. Regardless of whom or what you pray to, many have testified of the changes that it brings. Prayer does not need to be mystified, and no single religion or religious group should have autonomy over it.

Since life is not always a bed of sweet-smelling roses, sometimes we need help to get through the rose-filled but thorny maze of which none of us are exempt from feeling the piercing of those thorns. In the moments when we feel the weakest, prayer can help to revive purpose within us. Prayer allows us to communicate with a source that we understand can help us get through it. For those who are not interested in religion or spirituality, prayer may look like self-talk. For some, meditation is a form of that prayer. All I know, there were times in my life that I fell to my knees, praying as tears flood my face.

My prayer does not have to look like yours. People pray in different ways, and although prayer may mean different things to the individual, the goal is pretty much the same – to connect with a source of hope, life, and healing. We all experience burdensome and occasionally heart wrenching situations. Prayer can help, especially when you feel there is no one else to turn to for assistance. Perhaps it would help you better if you consider prayer as a conversation with your friend on the other end of the phone line - one who is supportive, free from pessimism, and afford guidance. As we travel this life, we will experience a host of conditions that we cannot explain but cannot endure alone.
Moreover, sometimes, the issues are too personal to share with us. In these times, prayer can help. Whether you believe in a deity, whatever you call it, her, him, or them. You can benefit from having that private communication.

Meditation

While I do not subscribe to any religion, one of the most defining moments in my life called for me to use all the tools in my life's toolbox, including prayer, to transition through the disappointment. Along with my journal writing, I had to use meditation to bring me back to calm and balancing by clearing my thoughts to remove all harmful residues from this experience. I could not depend on others for clarity. I needed to do this myself and by myself. Meditation helped to silent my busy mind while helping me to reconnect with my inner strength.

I am the fool.

I saw the writings on the wall, but I guess I prefer to be the victim because I did not walk away long before this situation got infested with crazy.

Excuses after excuses. I introduced my daughter to a new world. I moved her into a new life and changed her world without asking. Now its crumbled with its co-builder completely unremorseful or sympathetic. I did not want to fail.

I introduced her to a family. It was what I hoped to give her. For the first time, she had a sibling, but this was the second time I lived with a man. The first was her dad, my husband then…I walked away from its toxicity, only to discover that other relationships can get even more noxious.

How can I not have a pity party when I am the co-creator of this hot mess?

Do I deserve love?

Do I deserve to have functionality and reciprocation in a family that I can say is mine?

Do I deserve happiness?

Do I deserve a man who puts me first and understands my needs, doing whatever it takes to meet those desires?

Do I truly deserve to have trust, support, love, and laughter?

Or, am I doomed to the eternal loop of emotional struggle, dysfunction, pain, and disrespect?

How can a man I sacrificed so much for push me to the ground in front of another woman? The same way he could look me into my eyes and tell me he did not need me as much as I needed him or that I was useless.

Why did I still stick around?

Why did I do that?

Why did I not leave?

I mostly wanted to prove to myself and others who said it would not work that I could have a healthy, thriving relationship.

I wanted to give my daughter more than what I had taken from her.

Instead, I messed up at greater levels and put even my health at higher risks.

Now, I am pregnant, wondering if he even cares. Pregnant by someone who makes it clear I am easily replaced. He did not hesitate to have her in the same spot that I once laid, which got me thinking that I, too, laid in the exact spot that someone else did.

I was not ever special to him.

I was just another pawn, and I was warned but determined to see another side. I was wrong.

One of the symptoms of emotional trauma is that of self-pity. For a person who is already wounded internally, it is easy to become excessively self-absorbed with the idea of doing something or making a poor choice. Repeatedly, we obsessed over all the things we should have done differently, and the thought that we are only to blame becomes stuck in our heads. We internalize others' actions as our sole responsibility, and for a period, all we do is bombard our minds and antagonize our emotions with self-doubting thoughts. When famous or influential people commit suicide, many are shocked, especially if they appear benevolent and positive. In 1987, Primo Levi, an Italian Jewish chemist, writer, and Holocaust survivor. He was the author of several books, novels, collections of short stories, essays, and poems, which often relayed a courageous message of dignity and hope in the face of a cruel and senselessly tragic world. His death left his admirers bereft and baffled. Regardless of who you are or what region of the world you live in, the stress of the world can become all-encompassing and can swiftly overcome us all unless we instill practices that will still our minds and bring us back to balance.

Regardless of who you are or where you live, the stress of the world can be all-encompassing. It can overcome you unless you embrace practices that keep your mind and bring you back to balance. Along with our personal experience, our environment also contributes to the condition of our mind and our overall health - long drives and congested commutes; constant multi-tasking and addiction to social media; the continuous pursuit of love and money, and the pressure to compete with the next Instagram model. Living in a fast-paced metropolis make stress is inevitable. Meditation can keep us sane. The regular practice of quieting your mind has profound effects on your behaviors and even your creativity. Russell Simmons is a successful businessman and philanthropist with several different companies. He is always on the go but makes time for meditation daily. He encourages entrepreneurs to participate for at least twenty minutes a day.

In his blog, "Russell Simmons: 3 Simple Ways Meditation Will Make You a Better Entrepreneur," he offers three strong reasons to make meditation part of our routine:

1. Focus – meditation sharpens our minds by allowing us to release trapped emotions and let go of the distractions that have fogged our thoughts.
2. Balance- mediation enables us to put failure and successes into perspective. It keeps us present in the moment to better embrace the process instead of focusing on results to significantly improve our quality of life.
3. Creative – meditation allows us to tap into our creative selves by becoming still and one with our inner thoughts. In that stillness, we can tap into innovative ideas that typically gets clouded by our busy lifestyles.

With time, I could no longer justify carrying around toxic emotions that affected my perception of self and my relationship with others. Meditation became the best practice for regulating my thoughts and keeping me grounded. Moreover, it relieved the anxiety that caused me to expect something terrible would happen when things were going well and manage my high blood pressure triggered by my recent batch of stress. I would meditate at different times of the day because it improved my mindfulness. I no longer wanted to live a life of panic or anxiety. I wanted change.

During summer 2017, I completed Oprah and Deepak's 21-Day Meditation Experience. It was a commitment and journey that I am glad I embarked upon because it introduced me to silent mantra meditation. It was well needed. Each day, Oprah gave an intention for the day, then Deepak led the 20-minute meditation session. It had no religious affiliation, and believers and non-believers alike practice it. The techniques presented were effortless. Each day as Oprah started the session with words of guidance and inspiration, I took notes of what she said and journaled my thoughts. Journal writing is another great practice for healing from emotional traumas that I will address later. In the process of participating in the meditation, I truly experienced an opening in my senses. There were days I recalled just releasing memories that I did not realize I even had and was a spiritual cleanse for me - 21 days of healing from within. I was more grounded, and even my body received a recharge.

Benefits of Meditation

People fear what they do not understand, so although there are tons of empirical data to support the benefits of meditation, there are still those who will not practice it. They believe it goes against their spiritual construct. Nevertheless, hundreds of research shows how meditation improves the lives of those with PTSD or other health impairments. Combined with healthy eating and routine activities, the results of the studies are generally fascinating.

In its journal "Hypertension," the American Heart Association reported that the meditation practice had shown to lower blood pressure. A five-year study of patients with coronary heart disease reported a 48% reduction in heart attack, stroke, and death among those practicing this meditation technique. The Journal of Human Stress found that there was a significant reduction in cholesterol levels when people practiced meditation. Interestingly, these health results surpassed that of any controlled group, even when the same health education on eating right and exercise. The study, published in "Stroke," found that those who learned the Transcendental Meditation technique showed reduced the carotid artery's thickening. In contrast, the control group continued thickening of this artery. (Transcendental Meditation, n.d.)

With permission, students at a local school could participate in a 15-minute meditation, an eye-opening experience for them. Students appeared receptive to the concept of freeing their minds without being attached to their phones. It was fascinating to watch students who were typically disruptive, sitting at ease in silence. Throughout the year, work load and various situations stress students and teachers out alike. They are juggling a full school day and a hefty workload. For many, it seems like there is no downtime. The stress level is causing mental fatigue and limiting the quality of learning. As so many school districts are realizing, this is a good reason to introduce meditation into schools.

ADHD researchers report "a dramatic reduction in stress, anxiety, and depression," and meditation has effectively replaced the use of medication for students and people with PTSD disorders. While drugs for ADHD has caused several medical issues, meditation has provided calm for students, improving their behavioral and academic performance.

Students who participated in meditation claimed it was refreshing, and they felt more relaxed, which helped them feel less impulsive. Meditation is a simple act that students can do, but it delivers an immense impact. We must teach our children how to control their minds. There should be an emphasis on self-regulation, often achieved through meditation. All children can benefit from meditation, even those who do not have an attention deficit, since it lowers blood pressure and increases focus.

"It is vital that we start addressing the high levels of emotional stress being reported by high school and college students. Decreased stress can have a positive impact on mental health, and can also reduce the risk for hypertension, obesity, and diabetes—major risk factors for heart disease."
- Dr. Charles Elder, M.D., lead author of the TM study, and investigator at Kaiser Permanente Center for Health Research

With the increase in school violence, Dr. Charles Elder, M.D., lead author of the Transcendental Meditation study and investigator at Kaiser Permanente Center for Health Research, stresses the importance of reducing stress levels within students. Some students are prisoners of their environment, and meditation can free them from the inside. Transcendental Meditation is a highly researched type of meditation that is simple and effortless so that anyone can practice it. It is a silent technique, which involves sitting for about twenty minutes

70

with your eyes closed. You can practically do this anywhere. Meditation does not have to have anything to do with spirituality, but it is about mindfulness, stilling your thoughts, and permitting yourself to create a positive mindset.

How to Meditate

There are courses available that teach how to meditate. For me, simplicity is key. Whenever steps are overly complicated, it can quickly become overwhelming. Here doctors are more pharmaceutical drugs inclined; however, since I prefer to live a more holistic life, I was committed to this simple method of relaxing my mind and body. The act of meditation itself can be quite simple.

Basic Start:
Where you are standing or sitting, take ten deep breaths. Breathe in. Breathe out and relax.
It will help you to put things in perspective, whether you are feeling conflicted or just upset. Do not increase your heart rate or blood pressure by stressing over anything that you cannot control.

My Routine
1. Walk up around 5 AM - the quietest times of the day for me when my daughter and pets are still asleep. It is noiseless outside, and I appreciate the stillness.
2. My music app is set to namaste or relaxing music. Typically, I only listen to music when my mind is too busy.
3. Set the timer for 20 minutes.
4. Sit in a comfortable place, preferably on my yoga mat facing the window in the lotus "crisscross apple sauce" position.
5. Taking deep breaths, I release thoughts that are conflicting, confusing, or purely negative. I do not get fixated on any one thought but instead, allow my thoughts to flow freely. If the mind is extremely foggy, I will repeat a personal mantra.

After meditation, I like to go outside and run. It is liberating. Even when I am struggling to put one foot before the other, my mind in a

71

clear state says, "No ma'am. You have a goal to accomplish. Keep going." I have a mixture of distilled water with lemon, lavender, peppermint, and eucalyptus essential oils in a spray bottle. Throughout the day, whenever I feel overwhelmed, I misted myself with this blend. At work, I spray the room, dim the lights, and play relaxing music since I cannot always sit in a meditative position. Having a routine that contributes to my calm has had a significant impact on my performance. You can set the emotional climate wherever you are. At work, set the ambiance to promote an environment conducive to peace while thinking about what brings you a sense of calm. It could be a picture, a smell, or a sound that brings you to a that takes you there. Someone once told me that he tries to recreate the atmosphere of home at work to maintain self-control and overall sanity teaching his high school students.

Meditation is a way to give yourself a break, an honest break from all the hustle and bustle. It allows you to get outside of your head while permitting you to show yourself compassion. I have found that it is an essential tool to rejuvenate the mind and body. When someone decides that there needs to be a change in their life and habits, they recognize that change begins within. Nothing will happen until we become still and connect with who we are on the inside. Meditation introduced to students have shown improvement in their memory and overall performance, teachers' capacity to plan and organize; while helping inmates and veterans to feel empathy.

Music Therapy

Battling the idea that I was pregnant by a man that I was no longer in a relationship with and unwilling to consider an abortion. I found refuge in one song that I repeatedly played for days - "I am Light" by India Aria. The song came at precisely the right time when I needed it and spoke directly to my inner self. Although the song was of few words, it spoke to exactly what I was experiencing. I determined to call my son a derivative of the word Light. These are some of the words that spoke loudest to me:

72

I am not the things my family did
I am not the voices in my head
I am not the pieces of the brokenness inside
I am light
I am light
I'm not the mistakes that I have made or any of the things that caused me pain
I am not the pieces of the dream I left behind

People have used music's lyrics and vibrations to motivate, inspire, and relax them since the beginning of time. Music is therapeutic for some and motivational for others. Some people use music to get them pumped up for hardcore workouts, while others use it to get through their day. It is not surprising then that there is a genre of therapy using music. Music therapy is the use of music to improve a person's quality of life. It is an evidence-based, clinical use of music interventions where the therapist uses music to improve their clients' health and quality of life. Music therapists help clients by using different methods to treat their emotional and other needs.

There are two basic types of music therapy: receptive and active, also called expressive music therapy. While receptive music therapy guides patients or clients in listening to live or recorded music for their treatment, active music therapy engages them in creating music using their voice or instruments. Receptive music therapy helps with coping skills that consistently improve mood, decrease stress, pain, anxiety level, and enhance relaxation. Listening to India Arie's "I Am Light" acted as receptive music therapy for me.

Music therapy is effective when used with adolescents in treating mood/anxiety disorders, eating disorders, inappropriate behaviors, substance abuse, and may even help reduce suicide attempts. Goals in treating adolescents most at risk with music therapy include recognition and awareness of emotions and moods, improved decision-making skills, opportunities for creative self-expression, decreased anxiety, increased self-confidence, improved self-esteem, and better listening skills.

73

(Music therapy, n.d.)

Diet and Exercise

You are what you eat. If your food is not contributing to your peace of mind and your life's quality, do not consume it because having a healthy body improves your chances of dealing with stresses or other traumas. Find the foods that work best for you. However, reducing sodium and processed foods, increasing earth foods, and drinking enough water are paramount. Trauma disrupts our body's natural balance, freezing us in a state of hyperarousal and fear – meaning, we are always looking for something to go wrong or walking around with a chip on our shoulders. Exercise can bring us back to our natural equilibrium as we burn off unused adrenaline and release hormones that will make us feel happy.

Find an activity that you like to do that involves the whole body. Set up doable times and commit to moving at least three times a week for more than 30 minutes each day. If you are a gym member with group classes, those are highly encouraged because you do not focus on the discomfort of working out as much. Group classes are enjoyable because I have instruction and like-minded people to keep me motivated throughout my workout. Be conscious about what your body is doing to prevent or reduce the chances of injury and increase your chances for optimal results. Additionally, your diet and exercise can help you sleep better to assist in needed coping skills.

Healthy and Reciprocal Relationships

The ultimate purpose is to heal from emotional traumas to engage in healthy relationships that facilitate happiness. To do this requires a level of emotional intelligence to recognize when something needs fixing. Although there are times we go through life on autopilot, unaware of what is causing us to hurt or inflict pain, maturity means making conscious efforts towards our awareness. Pain

74

is an indication that something is wrong. For anything to change, we must admit that there is a problem, then take the necessary steps to find its source. Honestly, too many of us live disconnected from our emotions, so we waste time indulging in mindless or emotional numbing activities. Being emotionally intelligent allows us to reconnect and gather tools to assist in our emotional mending. An emotionally intelligent person practices self-management and self-awareness to improve the relationship they have with themselves and others.

Healing is bringing yourself to a state of health after internal or external damage has taken place. It is not temporary. Once healing is complete, it is in a solid-state, but it takes a process. There is no shortcut in the process of healing. Depending on the wound, time alone will not heal. You may suppress the pain associated with the injury or even forget about it, but the sore remains or worsens unless appropriately treated. One sure way to facilitate healing is to surround yourself with people who have your best interest at heart. We are not an island, no matter how much we proclaim independence. The human experience is about relationships since we discover so much about our inner self based on these interactions. We need others. While there are times that you must build on your own, having a support network is an essential part of recovering.

In my immediate family, I am the eldest sibling of five children. I have three sisters and a brother. Ironically, I grew up feeling like an only child. Even in adulthood, the sense of being alone always surrounded me, no matter how many people were in the room. Somewhere in my upbringing, there began a disconnect, yet I continued to yearn for a family of my own. I have forged some solid relationships with people I call friends with time, but like anything else, the experiences have been bitter-sweet. At the core of it, though, I have realized that people are most vulnerable when they feel like they have no one to turn to for support. For a person recovering from emotional trauma, that sense of isolation can be detrimental to their progress and overall health.

My view of the world and relationships is not the same as everyone I meet. Environment and exposure contribute to the differences, yet

75

forgiveness, understanding, acceptance, and effective communication are fundamental in bridging our gaps and components of any growing relationship. Those recovering from trauma may go through life with the idea that there is a conspiracy against them, holding on to the belief that everybody is out to get them, making it hard to trust even those with good intentions. They operate from survival mode because they feel they must protect themselves. While their fears may be irritational to others, to them, their vigilance is justifiable. It is crucial that people who choose to love a broken person remain patient as they learn to trust.

Conflicts are inevitable in any relationship. However, when we speak sincerely with an ear to understand, we can resolve many disputes. Stephen R. Covey, the author of 7 Habits of Highly Effective People, says, "Seek first to understand, then to be understood." When you value people, you do not treat them poorly or if they are dispensable. Instead, you spend time learning them with little judgment. When someone has experienced betrayal, it is difficult but not impossible for them to trust, again. We are all diverse with different experiences and varying levels of trauma, so we perceive the world uniquely. Learn to accept people for who they are. They will grow and heal as they understand that you are there to help and not to bring harm.

Communication is king to rebuild any broken relationship. Furthermore, we must acknowledge when we are wrong and apologize. In its simplest definition, an apology means showing remorse for doing something wrong or causing an offense. Through self-analysis, we know when we should ask for forgiveness. Self-management means controlling impulsive behaviors and managing emotions well. For instance, instead of serial texting someone or calling them out of their names, we know when to put the phone down or to walk away in silence. Alternatively, the journal writes your thoughts or compose that text message without sending it. Since, at times, we struggle with adapting to changing circumstances, a good rule of thumb to follow is never to speak or do anything when you are angry. Even in tempestuous moments, managing our emotions well could mean the difference between preserving a relationship and destroying it.

Relationships are two-way streets, so developing an awareness of other people's needs and concerns is advantageous. Listen to understand and speak to others with respect so that they can understand you. To manage ourselves well in various situations means being consciously aware of our emotions affect our thoughts and behaviors. Regrettably, our insecurities, believing every negative thought that come into our heads, impatience, and the inability to manage what we say in conflicts can destroy relationships. A significant part of healing depends on your surroundings. Some of us are functionally depressed, so we remain socially active without others realizing your darkness. Although isolation can worsen the feelings attached to internal trauma, being around the wrong people can intensify the pain in the same way. Do your best to connect with others authentically. Be aware of those who want to exploit or degrade you without the need to be hypervigilant or paranoid. Know when to walk away from people who have shown you they are not good for you.

Replace negative emotions with positive ones. Engage in social activities that are fun and bring your laughter. When you are alone, listen to music, watch a comedy, journal write to release negative emotions. Ensure that you are around people you trust and with whom you feel safe. In addition to social activities, find ways to give back to others who may be suffering as much as you. Volunteer as much as possible at a shelter or somewhere that needs a helping hand. Helping someone else brings healing into your own life. It will also remind you of your strengths and reduce the focus of anything that may have bombarded your happiness. In so doing, you will meet new people who may have commonalities to start creating new memories.

Assembling with Like-Spirited People

In retrospect, being involved in church at an early age assisted in healing in those younger days. I got involved early and even got water baptized at nine years old. I often found relief in the spiritual learning concepts and had little prejudices towards who educated me, from

Rastafarian, Jehovah's Witness to Mormons. One of my earliest enlightened memories involved me sitting outside under the trees in our yard. It was heavenly to watch the branches of the smile at that memory because it was just me out, the clear sky, sway in what I considered worship. It was my hope in the unseen that kept me going even when things looked grim.

I survived poverty. I survived the lack of food, being without necessities, and wondering where I will sleep next. Times were tough, but there was this underlying peace. It was what I needed to make it through to the next phase of my life. Today, I recognize that all things worked together for my good. Church nurtured the spiritual need of me as a child trying to navigate the world.

Years spent in the church were by choice and no act of coercion on my parents' parts. There was an inherent desire to connect with Higher Power, which my environment instilled within me early on. Being among people who were on a path of spiritual enlightenment kept me. As I grew, I became mote involved in different areas of the church. I was a praise dance, youth leader, street evangelist, and Sunday School teacher. It was my outlet. Although today I do not identify as a mainstream Christian, those days created deep roots leading towards holistic healing.

Journal Writing

During my most recent 21-day meditation with Oprah and Deepak, I took notes each day to reflect on the message presented in subsequent days. Journal writing was already part of my habit, and I found solace in sharing my joys or heartbreak with my book friend. I started each entry with a list of things I was thankful for that day before going into anything else.

Journal writing is said to be the oldest and most widely practiced form of self-help. Keeping a personal journal or diary is a way for you to record your most meaningful thoughts and feelings. It is an excellent way to release trapped emotions, especially if you are a private person and prefer no one to know your troubles. Interestingly, it can also give you clarity in a unique way. Writing allows us an opportunity to manage our emotions through self-reflection, which often minimizes the impact of the momentous event that we had once found most upsetting. Of course, depending on what happened, our emotions will influence the writing; however, instead of becoming overwhelmed with emotions, rational thinking shares the space.

Studies suggest that writing about traumatic, stressful, or emotional events triggers physical and psychological health improvements. (Baikie, Wilhelm, & y, 2005) Writing then is a type of therapy. My intention for writing this book was to help others heal through emotional trauma, and it became therapeutic for me. In shifting my focus, I was able to release the stress of dealing with a pregnancy loss, the uncertainty of my relationship, the discomfort of my changing health and channel into creativity. Everyone is prone to troubling and conflicting thoughts. Through the act of writing in this way, you can put a brake on those thoughts to open your consciousness, broaden your paradigm, and experience relief.

21-Day Meditation Journal Entry

On July 13, 2018, I joined millions worldwide on the 21-day Meditation with Oprah Winfrey and Deepak Chopra. The experience was titled "Manifesting Grace through Gratitude" to help participants alleviate stress, revitalize their psyche while finding their real source of joy within every moment without chasing the illusion of things we think need to be happy. Each day, I journal my experience. I have included my journal entries to give you an insight into what I gained during that time. It is also a guide to how you can journal your thoughts later in the book when you complete your journal writing activity.

Day 1 – Energy of Attraction
You attract who you are with your energy and intentions. Fear causes anger. Love produces joy, and thoughts create things. We create our own experiences by who we are. Ask for what you desire and expect to receive them. Our intentions influence our desire to achieve any results—basically, my life progress through my passions. Therefore, my inner intentions and desires must cooperate and align with each other.

Day 2 – Laws of the universe
The laws of the universe are neutral. They are unbiased and impartial, so regardless of religious affiliations, conscious or unconsciousness, acknowledgment, or ignorance, they work. They do not take sides. The goal is to ask for our inner intentions and circle of desires to be positive and life-supporting so that we can continue to attract positive results even when a situation looks negative. While we can have passive intentions, desires are active. They are a creative act that works on your behalf to gain what you have in your purposes. You will earn nothing without stepping out and doing something.

One of the pivotal points that I took from this day is not being judgmental towards myself and my desires. Sometimes, we tell ourselves that our desires are too grandeur, which prevents us from doing anything about achieving them. The idea is to become skillful, self-managing, free from emotional sabotage to get what you want without the pressure from your insecurities. Your desires should be life-supporting to bring you closer to fulfilling your designed purpose. Your desires should make you feel alive! It should excite you.

Day 3 – Desires
You know your desires are real when it is about being and not just about doing or gaining something. When you are present in the moment and when you are evolving as a human being, not one always busy doing something to feel important or trying to gain something to prove your significance. Your life supporting desires should align with your purpose to be the best you can be as a contributing citizen of the world.

On this day, I realized that for me to fulfill my desires or get what I truly wanted that I had to recognize my true self and then allow it to align with the universe's desires for my life. Through meditation, I began to tap into the truth that within me is the answers that I seek. Childhood or other emotional traumas do not taint my true self, nor is it limited by my fears or insecurities. My true self has unlimited potential. If I can stay connected to her, I can live the human experience that I most desire.

Day 4 – Effortless Creation
When I align my true self with the universe, and God, my desires will come effortlessly. Life is not supposed to be hard, so surrender. Whomever or whatever you hold dear to you, let them go. Release them. Set them free, and if they are purposed to remain with you, they will come back. Many times, we force things because we want what we want now, so we suffocate the life out of it. Surrender to a state of detachment that is not the same as indifference. You can care and love but be attached to nothing and connected to everything.

Some guru suggests that life is like a river and that we should be open to whatever happens. Once we align with our true selves, we will know what to do with whatever event presents itself.

Our true self contains our true passions, pure intentions, real desires, and authentic personality. There is no fake it until you make it. We put up the pretense to impress others, avoid addressing our reality, or because we are attached to the wrong things. Our disconnect from what is most important is causing additional hardship internally. Effortless creation happens without convincing or coercion.

Day 5 – Fulfillment of Desires
Society taught us to always look to an external source for answers, we often neglect to direct our attention within - search and locate our core beliefs and who we are. Can you answer the question, "Who Am I?" without listing all your accomplishments? My true self is worthy. She is

enough, whole, and complete. When I believe this about myself, I can then align with the universe for the effortless creation of my desires.

We spend so much time lying about who we are that we have convinced ourselves that we are something that we are not. Those untruths that we tell ourselves daily create internal conflicts because we say one thing but behave another way. Only your hidden intentions will attract into your life what you secretly desire. Again, you cannot manipulate the system or fake it. If you see conflicting situations showing up in your life, you may need to become more honest about what you are and what you want.

For example, we all want love. I have often struggled with keeping long-lasting relationships, although my deepest desires are to have them. I have realized that trapped unresolved emotions have caused a disconnect between and my pure self. While my true self is working on my behalf to bring into my life people who appreciate and support me, the hurt me who wants seeks isolation and protection, creating a contradiction that makes the manifestation of my desires difficult.

I deserve a man who asks for my hands and commits to me.

One who remains loyal to the process of us growing.

I deserve a whole family that works and plays together -

a family that considers each other.

I deserve to be appreciated and valued.

Being an assertive and resilient individual often means that others do not expect me to deal with self-doubt and insecurities. I do. During this mediation session, I honestly had to check my perception of self, including my beauty, talent, and good enough to be loved and accepted. In essence, those self-judgments were a hindrance to connecting to the power source that facilitates positive results. Anything done out of fear will bring adverse outcomes.

With everything I knew about the Law of Attraction and thoughts becoming things, I was still surprised when certain things happened in my life as if I was not the co-creator of my life.

Day 7 – Wholeness
We chase so many things in this life: money, fame, lovers, things, but our true self desires that we become whole – connected to our authentic self to activate our true power. Interestingly, the desires aligned with the real us have a way of manifesting easily, signaling that we are indeed connected. Instead of the pursuit of fickle things, our goal should be to be a balance, well-rounded, and complete to attain fulfillment.

Day 8 – Master the art of desire
The key to turning a dream into reality lies in three elements: intentions, consciousness, and awareness. All three of these will elevate us to our higher selves that can expedite the manifestations of our desires. Remember, we are always creating whether we realize it or not. The goal is to build purposefully. Conscious intention makes the creative process more efficient, causing us to rise above the level of any problems or trauma to experience a new level of clarity. It is also important to note that while we are not Creators, we are indeed creators. I am the creator of my human experience, and my intentions hold the key to my fulfillment. I am the co-creator of my life.

Day 9 – I am pure unbounded awareness
At this point in the meditation series, I am the most relaxed. It was on this day that I cried during my silent meditation. As I repeated the given mantra, I allowed myself to let go into an awareness of my true self, the one who has been waiting for her reveal. This day, I became more conscious of myself and my surroundings and recognized that I can obtain my heart's desires if I remain true. I released fears, stresses, and concerns that had bound me.

Day 10 – Focus!
Direct those desires to be life-giving and soul-affirming. When we meet our true selves and connect authentically, we become more

deliberate about what we want. Our inner intentions become apparent, and there is less internal turmoil, which essentially sends less mixed messages to the universe. Whatever we set our sights on must breathe life into us and others. Do not compromise your worth or ask others to negotiate theirs. It is detrimental to focus on what you do not want. If you ponder on your relationships' disappointments or the failure of your career efforts, you will get more disappointments and failures. Remember, whatever you focus on expands.

Meditation allows you to meet and connect with your higher self. It is essential to maintain that connection between yourself and the Source. You cannot be lazy about your desires. They should motivate you daily. It takes sustained and faithful attention to bring your hopes to fruition. Create magic with pure awareness. Your focus takes concentration, yet concentration does not mean hard work and struggling. Despite the external programming, mediation is simply being aware of our conscious mind. The gap between all your thoughts, and the quiet place beneath all the noise of our all our thinking. Meditation trains our minds to concentrate easily to tap into our unbounded awareness – a reservoir of possibilities.

Day 11 – My awareness is infinitely adaptable
Your life is unfolding one event at a time, so you do not always see the bigger picture. Remember, though, whatever is happening to you is also happening for you. Free your mind from emotional attachments that bring burden and pain. Release the heavyweights from your heart to make room for freedom, the fluidity of awareness, and fullness. Being flexible or exercising flexible consciousness means being open-minded to realize the results that the universe is bringing to you even when you cannot at first understand it.

Day 12 – I manifest desires easily and naturally
Our beliefs and others' ability can impede our ability to gain from the endless and bountiful possibilities that the universe has in store. Manifesting what we desire means having universal compassion from our unbounded awareness, focus attention, and flexible consciousness.

I am the conscious master of my creation. Living a conscious lifestyle is inspiring.

Toxic relationships, drugs, alcohol, negative emotions such as anxiety, depression, and low self-esteem work against us and make it difficult to manifest our true desires. To address these, though, we must check our core beliefs because they guide our good or otherwise behaviors. Conversely, optimism, relaxation, flexibility, confidence grounded in humility, and conscious self-awareness give our desires the freedom to flow smoothly and naturally. I want to be happy. The events that occurred in my early childhood anchored some core beliefs that I had to address as an adult. Since my upbringing centered on poverty and lack, I had a core belief that my life had to be hard. On a subconscious level, I felt I did not deserve to enjoy the fruits of my labor, so I always held my breath when something positive happened. I often expected something to go wrong when all seemed well. I struggled to accept that anyone could love me without conditions.

Unless we deal with our core beliefs about ourselves, the world in which we live, and the people around us, we will consistently blame others for the situations in which we find ourselves. It takes courage to look at ourselves and face those undesirables about ourselves. In addressing those things, I had to remain nonjudgmental about my past, realizing my identity is not tied up entirely in my failures or shortcomings or brokenness. Through meditation, journaling, exercise, and pay attention to my diet, I have developed a confidence that all things work out for my benefit. Instead of succumbing to life's challenges, I am learning to use them to become stronger and better.

Do not resist the thoughts or sensations that you feel in any given situation. If it is painful, feel it. However, do not try avoiding uncomfortable emotions; instead of getting stuck in that painful state, flow with the energy. Do what is necessary to get from that sad state and allow the law of attraction to work on your behalf. My awareness is infinitely adaptable. Be open to adapt to changes that life brings you without being so hard on yourself. Be compassionate to yourself as you practice loving others.

Day 13 – Manifesting from the true self
I intend to align my awareness with the creative power of the universe.
My true self is a divinity that transcends the mind and body.
Connecting to the Source will combat loneliness as you co-create your
life. I choose to align with my true self or not, but my true self will
manifest what is best for me. It works for me always, but it expands
when I become more aware and align myself accordingly. It taps into
the intelligence of the universe.

Day 14 – Fulfilling my dreams fulfills my spirit
On this day, before I went into my meditation, I took a moment to
reflect on what I truly wanted -healthy, thriving relationships. To have
that, I knew that I to become a better manager of my emotions. I will
open my heart to everything possible. I want to attract better for my
life and not just material things. I am more than what the eyes see. I
desire peace.

Day 15 – Sharing your happiness
Life is better when you share it. Help to enhance other's happiness,
and in turn, it will affect your own. Let go of the ego. While the ego
can be useful as a defense mechanism, it is detrimental to healing and
growth. If we want to live harmoniously with others, we have to check
our egos at the door.

Share your talents and your gifts. If you are good at something, allow
others the chance to be inspired and motivated by it. Consider the
story of the Biblical prodigal son: Both had ten talents, one buried his,
but the other used them all. The first one buried them, thinking he
could preserve them, not realizing that he was killing his potential and
robbing others of his gifts.

Expand your desires to include others. Go beyond the ego because the
ego isolates you and prevents you and your true self from uniting. Ego
clash is a gap between the true self, your higher understanding, and the
personality we try to defend. The ego has a limited perspective. Go
beyond the ego and focus on your true self.

The happiness of others is my happiness.

Day 16 – Trusting Nature's Course
Before I went to sleep last night, I broke down in tears. I realized that I must write and share my story of being sexually assaulted as a baby. I still have negative emotions attached to it. The world is about "we/us," and not just "I." Open your heart to connect deeply with others of like-mindedness without imposing your path onto others. I forgive those who have hurt me, hoping that in time, they will become self-aware. My inner intentions wish them the best because their path is their path. I cannot change anyone's perceptions of themselves or about me. I wish everybody healing, knowing that their spiritual path is their own. Forgiveness is a decision and a lifelong process.

Day 17 – Say Yes to Life!
Trust the universe to bring joy and happiness. Let go of the resistance to life caused by worry and stress. Amplify your power of attraction and relax in it all. Life experiences can be fun if you understand that the universe knows what is right for you. Trust with a playful attitude and detach from the results because desperation and uptightness will bring about disappointments. Chill and have fun. Perform actions without regard for the fruit of that action. Just do it because it is the right thing to do. The ego will not allow you to play because it is always thinking about winning and losing. Think, the bigger picture is that it is all working out for your good.

Day 18 – Manifesting through Grace
Introduction to the Law of Attraction many years ago helped my personal development. Yet, I did not wholeheartedly believe that my thoughts created things because I allowed negative thoughts to consume my thoughts at times. Over the years, my awareness is assisting in monitoring my thinking. That has produced more favorable results. Since forgiveness is a gift I often give to others, I decided to forgive myself for my self-infliction, for holding on to the hurt and internalizing others' actions, for keep putting my heart at risk, and for not showing myself compassion. I had to forgive myself and extend

the same kindness to myself as I have so graciously given to others. I had to give and receive grace – divine grace.

Day 19 – Becoming a Co-Creator
I am at the final three days of this 21-day meditation, and I am genuinely excited. I am thrilled for the sessions to be over to restart it again on my own with these notes. My life is evolving, and I can feel the change. There has been a shift in mental and emotional well-being as life reminds me to remain flexible, let go of the attachment to the outcome, and to monitor my thoughts often.

I choose to align myself with my true self and the Higher Intelligence, knowing confidently that the universe sees the bigger picture, and all things are working together for my good. I believe that I am a co-creator with the Higher Intelligence, through grace, creating the best experiences for my life. For every action, there is an equal or more significant reaction. I shape my reality with the Source. Regardless of what others do to me or try to do, I can shape those happenings.

Today, I am expanding my awareness. I play a role in the design of my life, and my existence means something. Understanding that my existence contains love and beauty, I develop the humility to shrink my ego, align with the universe, and be part of the collective intelligence. I enjoy being a co-creator of my life.

Day 20 – Finding My Freedom!
I have grown, and I can tell. Today, I saw someone who recognized that change. I took it as affirmation for my spiritual progress and my evolution. I have always admired that I am willing to embrace transformation because I genuinely look forward to meeting the newer versions of me. With every decision, through every experience, and passing time, I discover new levels of me. I love the process, even when it does not always feel good. Today, I am flexing my mind, exercising my awareness to include newness, something fresh and different. I will not co-create anything that will bring me harm or reverse my progress.

I will realign with the universe, the Cosmic Intelligence, to fulfill my purpose of happiness. I am happy and grateful now.

Everything shared between all of us is in the realm of the spirit. We are love, and we are here to manifest love. If anything operates from a different place than love, it is not of our true self. Something that is not of you is influencing it. I am part of the spark that creates and shapes the universe as it is and will be. Although the ego has constricted awareness, meditation and other practices will allow me to tap into unbounded knowledge and limitlessness. Compulsions and distractions are a disruption to the natural flow. Self-awareness allows me to connect with my higher self so that my ego or desires do not trap me. I control all my compulsions and manifest my desire for freedom.

Day 21- My Presence Brings Peace
I have stuck to this 21-day meditation and have made it to this last day. While there has been a metamorphosis, some of my poor habits, personality flaws, and fears have remained. Above all things, I seek love and acceptance. I had to be kind to myself as I realized that migrating to another country, getting divorced from the person I moved with, and still developing my dreams take courage and much flexibility. Although I have grown so much, I know there is room for more growth.

I deserve to be appreciated and not taken for granted. I look forward to enjoying this human experience with someone who can accept me just as I am and not leave me for it. I desire to have a life partner who does use my personality to justify his bad behaviors. I deserve respect, passion, and a commitment from someone who does not treat me as an afterthought. Without desperation, I desire a family that I never had. One that I can call my own. One that exhibits the behaviors of trust, honor, love, laughter, creating awesome memories, unity, and just always being happy even when we are figuring out how to love each other. I dream of a reciprocal relationship. I want to love without conditions.

I am at peace – the place of being and not just doing – in harmony with who I truly am through grace and love. Here, I have an expanded awareness, a sense of enlightenment where my ego is left behind. I will live my truth because my presence creates peace. My presence brings peace and not confusion.

This activity was essential to my healing and growth. Although I used words such as "cosmic intelligence," it is important to note that it is interchangeable to whatever you recognize as a higher power source.

Chapter Summary/Key Takeaways

In this chapter, we explore different strategies to overcome emotional trauma and heal. The practices presented are practical and easy to maintain. Follow these often. We are not perfect people, but we can turn every pain into passion. The process may not be quick. However, taking the right steps is well worth it.

In the final chapter of this book, there nothing to read but everything to apply. You will use the pages provided to start your journey towards journal writing.

Be the spark you want to see
in the world.

Healing Emotional Traumas

On my journey towards healing, some of the most unexpected people were there to support me. It is not always the people you spend the most time with that will be there at the crucial turning point, or the people you call family who will stand in the gap when you need strength. Time and time again, it was the assistance of strangers that guided me through dark tides. When you get through, it is your turn to reach down, reach back, and help someone else. Sometimes, you cannot even wait to complete the process of healing before helping someone. Sometimes, it is in the process of helping someone else that brings about your complete healing.

There is no shortage of places to offer aid. Shelters are overflowing, schoolhouses, jail, and prison cells. People are looking for help. The night I was crouched over on all fours losing my only son, it was my hairstylist who came to my aide. There was no family or others that I called my closest friends. Although it was close to midnight, when I called, she answered. The paramedics went above and beyond to comfort me through one of the most agonizing nights of my life – strangers.

Honestly, while we all have experienced something sad or painful in our lives, we won't all have a traumatic disorder. Nevertheless, it is not up to you to decide what is a crisis for a person and what is not. If you can be there for them and if you can offer support, do so. If you cannot, you also have the freedom to walk away or refuse to help. You do not ever have to enable lousy behavior. At times it is necessary to leave the work up to professionals. In contributing to others, be mindful not to become overtaken by their negative emotions because it can be contagious.

When someone you love hurt, you hurt. Sometimes, your presence alone can help those people to recover emotionally. Do not be afraid to lend a helping hand. Of course, you are human, and there will be times where you feel you are in no position to be the best lending hand you can be. It may be a regrettable decision later, but at that moment, it is understandable that all of us must do what is in our best self-interest. Like the air, attendants always say, "Put on your mask first before helping others." You cannot help anyone else if you are unconscious or worst, so be mindful not to give too much of yourself, leaving you depleted.

In all things, choose patience and understanding. If someone trusts you enough to share their dismay with you, please listen without judgment. Confiding in someone else is not always easy because it is like reliving the pain each time. It takes time for people to heal. While you do not want to enable negative behaviors or prolong the anguish, be patient with others. Support them and help them to release the pain and move forward to living a more fulfilling life.

Be genuine in your support. Invite that person to social events that encourage relaxation and fun. Please do not force them to give you details of anything. They will talk to you when they feel comfortable to say. Just be there for them. Be a safety net. It is not personal. Remember that people respond to hurt in different ways. Some are quiet and withdrawn, while others become loud and angry. That could make you feel helpless or that they do not like you, but as mean as it may sound, this time is not about you. They need compassion and understanding but do not let them wallow in self-pity. Your love is vital through all of this. Love conquers all things. Love will always win, even when you must give distance for them to heal and grow.

It is essential to point out that children are little people, too. They are valuable. As we know, they also experience distasteful and unpleasant events. Speak sincerely to them to gain an insight into what is going on in their heads and hearts. With open communication, children can learn how to cope with the fear or upset from any possible traumatic event. If they observe adults dealing positively with their issues, they may be better able to work through their symptoms. Assist our most vulnerable to experience life in a more enlightened way.

Journal writing is genuinely enlightening. It is like having a personal sounding board that allows you to put circumstances into perspective. Some even turn their journaling into open letters or blogs.

Megan Ace and I attended Middlesex University together in England. She was always cheerful with the most mesmerizing eyes. Her personality was a delight. On-campus, in between classes, and during lunchtimes, we would hang out, but I did not know much more about her life. It was not until much later, when I moved to America, that I saw her heart. We stayed connected through social media, and I would saw her posts. Her writing was eloquent and detailed. Then two of them capture my attention. They were two open letters written to her parents. They were both beautiful, heartfelt, and tragic simultaneously.

In light of writing this book, Healing from Emotional Traumas, I decided to reach out to Megan. In that conversation, she permitted me to use the letters in my book to contribute to the most traumatic events in her life. I chose to use the one with her father because it truly captured the sense of relatable trauma, but many of us would prefer to avoid it. Megan used writing as therapy to help her through some of the roughest times in her life. She took her pain and turned it into something beautiful. Then, she shared it with the world.

Read Megan's letter to her father and allow them to help you heal through words. You can read the other letter to her mother on her blog, www.SelfishMother.com

Although her anger would have been justifiable, Megan expresses forgiveness in this open letter to release the years of pent-up disappointment and pain from her heart. Instead of becoming consumed by it all, she decided to use the tragedy as fuel for something greater. She let go of the hurt, which gave her more room for love. Healing chooses to be free from traumatizing strongholds, especially when the person who hurt you may never be in your life again.

A LETTER TO MY ALCOHOLIC DAD, WHO DIED WHILST I WAS GIVING BIRTH

Dear Dad,

Your drug and alcohol addiction, which lead you to your final destination and 'great escape', for me, made the arrival of my son, terribly hard to comprehend. After a very long and complicated birth, I too, was to experience the all-consuming drug, which had been your consumer, your master for so many years. I thought about you and for the first time, understood how it must have instantly transported you into what you thought was a happier place.

After my adoring, doting husband and my incredible mother, your ex wife, had gone home, I embraced my son with the warmth of a thousand suns and I thought of you. How proud you'd be of your only 'darling daughter' and your brand new, unspoilt grandson, merely hours old. In the face of sheer exhaustion and an overwhelming feeling of love, so raw, it's painful, I decided to share my news with you. Having not seen you since very early on in my pregnancy, I compose my message and send you the text. A text which you would never receive. A text which when your phone bleeps beside my mother's bed, she once again, would have to absorb my hope.

Unbeknown to me, you went into hospital as I did, during the early hours. My fatherly-like bothers and mum had asked my husband if he thought I should know of your situation and he, quite wisely, said no. Another impossible decision your addiction has made one of my loved ones make. I found out that you were upstairs, breathing via a machine the morning

96

after I had given birth. The wonderful nurses and midwives gave me the option of them taking me up on my bed to say my goodbyes and to hold your hand, for one last time. What devoted angels. I felt so lucky to be in their overwhelmingly precious and selfless care.

Sadly, my youngest of two brothers, your second son, was not to be so lucky in finding his peace with you. Travel, timings and the fact that his wife had given birth to their second son, your forth grandson, a mere four weeks' earlier, made it an impossible task for him to say goodbye (although the wonders of FaceTime, really are underestimated!). As my biggest brother, your eldest son, on his broadest of shoulders wheeled me to your bedside, I cannot for the life of me recall what I said to you. Only how I wish you could have met our King of a son, or at least known that he had arrived safely. I know you would have cared deep down inside, even if those battled demons wouldn't have allowed you to show us. There was of course humour too in that moment. How we find that in the most surreal situations, never ceases to amaze me.

As I get ready to give birth once more, I'm thankful that I won't have to endure the emotional ordeal of your death again. But I also know that none of it was your fault. Even through so many years of turmoil, manipulation and guilt, I have no blame. I'm sorry that you have missed out on so much – your three children, five grandsons and now a 6th grandchild on the way, and I'm sorry I couldn't have saved you. I witness such wonderful qualities of yours in all of your grandsons and I know how much they all would have been just as absorbed in your magical stories as the three of us were, and how richer their lives would be if you could have played a role in them.

I wish that you could know of your inheritance track which has been passed to my son and of the 'angels guarding him while he sleeps', just as you promised they always did for me. I wish you were alive and I wish you hadn't been an addict.

Angels guard you, Dad. X
P.S. It's a girl.

Forgiveness is for you, not for the other person. However, it does affect the quality of the relationship you have with others.

Personal Journal Entry

For any information in this book to work for you, you must apply it to your life. Personalize the messages to your specific circumstances to meet your personal needs. Make it practical and applicable. The remainder of this chapter is devoted to the idea that 21 days create a habit. These days will be divided into three phases of seven days each for optimum results.

For these first seven days, journal the most traumatizing moment or an event that has hurt you the most. Each day after you write, meditate, or get active. Complete this seven-day journal walk and repeat the process three more times to form a new journal writing habit. Pick the best times to write, either first thing in the morning or before you go to bed at night. Each day end your writing with the statement, "I am loved, cherished, respected, protected, and safe."

Phase 1 – The Decision Is Just the Beginning

Day 1

_____

_____

_____

_____

_____

_____

_____

_____

_____

_____

_____

_____

_____

_____

_____

Day 2

_____

_____

_____

_____

_____

_____

_____

_____

_____

_____

_____

_____

_____

_____

Day 3

_____

_____

_____

_____

_____

_____

_____

_____

_____

_____

_____

_____

_____

_____

Day 4

_____

_____

_____

_____

_____

_____

_____

_____

_____

_____

_____

_____

_____

_____

_____

Day 5

_____

_____

_____

_____

_____

_____

_____

_____

_____

_____

_____

_____

_____

_____

Day 6

_____

_____

_____

_____

_____

_____

_____

_____

_____

_____

_____

_____

_____

_____

Day 7

_____

_____

_____

_____

_____

_____

_____

_____

_____

_____

_____

_____

_____

_____

_____

You have completed your first phase of journal writing. Confronting your pain is not easy, but you are on your way to healing from emotional traumas. Although, at times, we prefer to mask the pain with distractions, alcohol, or drugs, the best way to heal is to expose the wound and dress it with appropriate solutions. Purposeful change happens when we are strategic about what we want to see a difference.

I am loved, cherished,
respected, protected, and safe.

Phase 2 – Commit to the Process

As you know, healing takes time. One day you feel like you are on top
of the world, and the next day you are struggling to keep your
optimism. For the next seven days, focus on only the positive. Each
day write down in great detail one good thing that happened during the
day. At the end of each entry, write, "I am happy and grateful now."

Day 1

_____

_____

_____

_____

_____

_____

_____

_____

_____

_____

_____

_____

_____

_____

Day 2

_____

_____

_____

_____

Day 3

Day 4

_____
_____
_____
_____
_____
_____
_____
_____
_____
_____
_____
_____
_____
_____
_____

Day 5

_____
_____
_____
_____
_____
_____
_____
_____
_____
_____
_____
_____
_____
_____

_____

_____

Day 6

_____

_____

_____

_____

_____

_____

_____

_____

_____

_____

_____

_____

_____

_____

_____

Day 7

_____

_____

_____

_____

_____

_____

_____

You are on a roll. You are 14 days into a changed mindset, and you are
well on your way to creating a new habit. Remember, the work
continues even after you do the work. There will be days that you just
want to sink into bad feelings. You simply do not want to exert the
effort required to enforce the practices you know that will pull you out
of the rot, but you must do it. It takes work, yet it gets easier the more
you incorporate behaviors that facilitate shifting your paradigm. Create
better habits for your recovery. Your perspective on what you have
been through will determine how well you heal from emotional
traumas so that you can stop sabotaging your happiness. Tomorrow is
gone. You only have today, right now. What are you going to do that
genuinely makes you feel good? It is crucial to keep in the forefront of
your mind that feeling good does not mean living in denial or masking
the pain. It means addressing it and doing what is best to help you
through to the next stage.

Today, you may need to go out dancing, do that. However, do not
overindulge in drinking that you are numb. Avoidance will only slow
down the healing process.

I am happy and grateful
now.

Phase 3 – Heal and Grow

Phase three marks the end of this book and the beginning of something fresh for you. As you walk away from this book, remember that you are a co-creator of your life. Your life is significant, and you contribute positively to everything around you. For this week, the goal is to think about your dreams and aspirations. Each day, write something about what you would like to accomplish, personal and professional. After each entry, write, "My presence brings peace."

Day 1

_____
_____
_____
_____
_____
_____
_____
_____
_____
_____
_____
_____
_____
_____

Day 2

_____
_____
_____

_____
_____
_____
_____
_____
_____
_____
_____
_____
_____
_____
_____
_____

Day 3

_____
_____
_____
_____
_____
_____
_____
_____
_____
_____
_____
_____
_____
_____
_____
_____

Day 4

_____

_____

_____

_____

_____

_____

_____

_____

_____

_____

_____

_____

_____

_____

_____

Day 5

_____

_____

_____

_____

_____

_____

_____

_____

_____
_____
_____
_____
_____
_____

Day 6

_____
_____
_____
_____
_____
_____
_____
_____
_____
_____
_____
_____
_____
_____
_____

Day 7

_____
_____
_____
_____
_____

_____

_____

_____

_____

_____

_____

_____

_____

_____

_____

L ife is not intended to be hard, but it is not sugarcoated, either. Your life is significant. Life can be messy, and we all have limitations from our personal experiences, emotions, and knowledge. However, regardless of what you have been through, now is your opportunity to use misfortunes to drive purpose. Use your gifts, your secret talents, no matter how trivial they may seem at first, to uplift and inspire others. As you continue to share who you are, you will grow in your abilities. Perfection is not the goal. You are human, so set your intentions on becoming the best person you can be despite the challenges and in the face of your fears. You are enough. Please do not take what others do personally because we are all on a journey. People are hurting, and sometimes, we become their casualty. Forgive them. Become the light you want to see around you with the belief that your presence brings peace and never confusion.

Healing is an ongoing process. As you keep living, you will pick up new tools to add to your resources to best deal with the inevitable cycle of life circumstances. Return to this book as needed, especially when you need a refresher.

Be blessed. Be a blessing.

My presence brings peace.

Epilogue

Healing is not an overnight event. It is a process that must be respected. Many of us have experienced situations that have left a deep scar on our hearts and minds. We must utilize the right strategies to help us recover from the trauma of these incidents. Meditation, forgiveness, and eating right are all effective means of getting us on the path of self-restoration. If you are dealing with something too painful to address by yourself, seek the assistance of professionals. You are not in this alone.

Bibliography

(n.d.). Retrieved from Transcendental Meditation:
https://www.tm.org/?leadsource=CRM662&utm_source=bin
g&utm_medium=cpc&utm_campaign=brand&msclkid=e03d2
52644cd12207408795ed541578a

Amstadter, A. B., & Vernon, L. L. (2008). Emotional Reactions During
and After Trauma: A Comparison of Trauma Types. *Journal of
Aggression, Maltreatment & Trauma, 16*(4), 391-408. Retrieved 2
7, 2019, from
https://ncbi.nlm.nih.gov/pmc/articles/pmc2800360

Baikie, K. A., Wilhelm, K., & y. (2005). Emotional and physical health
benefits of expressive writing. *Advances in Psychiatric Treatment,
11*(5). Retrieved 3 2, 2019, from
https://cambridge.org/core/journals/advances-in-psychiatric-
treatment/article/emotional-and-physical-health-benefits-of-
expressive-writing/ed2976a61f5de56b46f07a1ce9ea9f9f

Bardos, J., Hercz, D., Friedenthal, J., Missmer, S. A., & Williams, Z.
(2015). A National Survey on Public Perceptions of
Miscarriage. *Obstetrics & Gynecology, 125*(6), 1313-1320.
Retrieved 2 6, 2019, from
https://ncbi.nlm.nih.gov/pmc/articles/pmc4443861

Basics of Buddhism. (n.d.). Retrieved 2 7, 2019, from
https://www.pbs.org/edens/thailand/buddhism.htm

Bullying and Suicide. (n.d.). Retrieved 2 6, 2019, from Bullying Statistics:
http://www.bullyingstatistics.org/content/bullying-and-
suicide.html

CDC - Injury - Intimate Partner Violence Consequences. (n.d.). Retrieved 5
17, 2019, from National Center for Injury Prevention and
Control, Centers for Disease Control and Prevention:
https://www.cdc.gov/violencePrevention/intimatepartnerviol
ence/consequences.html

Druker, J. (2005). *On the Dangers of Reading Suicide into the Works of Primo
Levi.* Retrieved 5 21, 2019, from
https://link.springer.com/chapter/10.1057/9781403981592_2
0

Emotion. (n.d.). Retrieved 2 9, 2019, from Wikipedia: The Free
Encyclopedia: http://en.wikipedia.org/wiki/Emotion

Emotional and Psychological Trauma. (n.d.). Retrieved 2 9, 2019, from
    http://www.helpguide.org/mental/emotional_psychological_t
    rauma.htm
Forgiveness. (n.d.). Retrieved 5 20, 2019, from Wikipedia: The Free
    Encyclopedia: http://en.wikipedia.org/wiki/Forgiveness
Gordon, S. (2018, September 21). *What Are the Effects of Cyberbullying?*
    Retrieved from Very Well Family:
    https://www.verywellfamily.com/what-are-the-effects-of-
    cyberbullying-460558
Grief counseling. (n.d.). Retrieved 5 20, 2019, from Wikipedia: The Free
    Encyclopedia: http://en.wikipedia.org/wiki/Grief_counseling
Image. (n.d.). Retrieved 2 28, 2019, from Wikipedia: The Free
    Encyclopedia:
    http://commons.wikimedia.org/wiki/File:Sivakempfort.jpg
Kelleher, I., Harley, M., Lynch, F., Arseneault, L., Fitzpatrick, C., &
    Cannon, M. (2008). Associations between childhood trauma,
    bullying and psychotic symptoms among a school-based
    adolescent sample. *British Journal of Psychiatry, 193*(5), 378-382.
    Retrieved 2 6, 2019, from
    https://ncbi.nlm.nih.gov/pubmed/18978317
Kirmayer, L. J., Lemelson, R., & Barad, M. (2007). *Understanding
    Trauma: Introduction: Inscribing Trauma in Culture, Brain, and Body.*
    Retrieved 2 7, 2019, from
    http://assets.cambridge.org/97805218/54283/excerpt/978052
    1854283_excerpt.pdf
Learn the Transcendental Meditation Technique – Seven Step Program. (n.d.).
    Retrieved 2 28, 2019, from Tm.org: http://www.tm.org/learn-
    meditation
Meditation. (n.d.). Retrieved 2 28, 2019, from Wikipedia: The Free
    Encyclopedia: http://en.wikipedia.org/wiki/Meditation
Miller, E. (2010). Healing Developmental Trauma: A Systems
    Approach to Counseling Individuals, Couples and Families.
    Journal of Prenatal and Perinatal Psychology and Health, 25(1), 62.
    Retrieved 2 8, 2019, from
    https://questia.com/library/journal/1p3-2431676091/healing-
    developmental-trauma-a-systems-approach-to

Moore, A. A. (n.d.). *What is cyberstalking?* Retrieved 5 18, 2019, from About.com: http://womensissues.about.com/od/violenceagainstwomen/f/Cyberstalking.htm

Music therapy. (n.d.). Retrieved 5 21, 2019, from Wikipedia: The Free Encyclopedia: http://en.wikipedia.org/wiki/Music_therapy

Painter, R. M. (2009). *Healing Personal History: Memoirs of Trauma and Transcendence.* Retrieved 2 8, 2019, from https://link.springer.com/chapter/10.1007/978-1-4020-9802-4_10

Pettalia, J. L., Levin, E., & Dickinson, J. (n.d.). Cyberbullying: Eliciting harm without consequence. *Computers in Human Behavior, 29*(6), 2758–2765. Retrieved 2 6, 2019, from http://www.sciencedirect.com/science/article/pii/S07475632 13002586

Stress. (n.d.). Retrieved 5 14, 2019, from Wikipedia: The Free Encyclopedia: http://en.wikipedia.org/wiki/Stress_(biology)

Syeed, S. A. (2015). Sylvia Plath and her Inner World. *International Journal of Multifaceted and Multilingual Studies, 2*(1). Retrieved 5 21, 2019, from http://ijmms.in/sites/ijms/index.php/ijmms/article/view/22 4/212

Valdez, C. E., & Lilly, M. M. (2012). Emotional Constriction and Risk for Posttraumatic Stress: The Roles of Trauma History and Gender. *Journal of Aggression, Maltreatment & Trauma, 21*(1), 77-94. Retrieved 2 25, 2019, from http://tandfonline.com/doi/abs/10.1080/10926771.2012.631 165

What is Child Trauma. (n.d.). Retrieved from The National Child Traumatic Stress Network: https://www.nctsn.org/what-is-child-trauma

Writing therapy. (n.d.). Retrieved 3 2, 2019, from Wikipedia: The Free Encyclopedia: http://en.wikipedia.org/wiki/Writing_therapy

All photos contributed by Marsha Kerr Talley
Book cover design by Maduranga

Acknowledgments

Special thanks to Cortney Lancaster, Megan Ace, Stephanie Strike, my 2019 senior students, those who wished to remain anonymous, and all others who contributed to this book's completion. Your belief in healing is impressive, and your stories have inspired me to keep writing. I appreciate all of you and wish you the very best on your journey.

To the strangers, family members, and friends who have prayed with and for me, those who sent warm-heartfelt messages, and to those who showed up when I needed them the most, thank you. I appreciate you, all of you. Your gestures of care have not gone unnoticed. Thank you.

Special thanks to all who have caused me pain. You who smiled in my face but was a dagger in my back. Those of you who took my tolerance, patience, kindness, even resilience for granted. You who saw my pain and tears but chose your self-interest over showing sincere concern. I thank you. Without you, my life would have been less eventful; my potential to push through and become greater would have remained buried without your contribution.

To my daughter, Sky, you are my sunshine. You give me hope when I am feeling down. You are a beautiful soul, and I am so blessed to have you in my life.

To my Light. Thank you for coming to me. Return to me some time.

About the Author

Marsha Kerr Talley is an educator, public speaker, entrepreneur, and proud mother. Her childhood was one of much pain that propelled her into survival mode. However, she has managed to use her experiences to inspire others while developing herself in various capacities.

Kerr Talley was born in Kingston, Jamaica where she attended elementary and the first two years of high school. She completed high school in London, England. After a gap year, she finished college and attended Middlesex University receiving Bachelor of Arts degree. After getting married, she moved to Texas, United States. There she earned a Master of Science degree. Kerr Talley is currently pursuing a doctorate in education with principal certification.

In 2017, Kerr Talley self-published her first book, The Decision Is Just the Beginning, a personal development guide towards helping people pursue lifelong goals. Her purpose is to write self-help books that encourage readers to turn their pain into passion. As an instructional leader in the public-school setting and working with students from diverse backgrounds, language proficiency, and learning disabilities, she has obtained a depth of knowledge that helps her students and others around her.

Kerr Talley is also a public figure using social media to talk about controversial and self-helping issues. Visit her website, www.MarshaKerrTalley.com.

I am light.